31 Days of Prayer for my Children

D1360042

BroadStreet
PUBLISHING

BroadStreet Publishing® Group, LLC
Savage, Minnesota, USA
BroadStreetPublishing.com

31 Days of Prayer for My Children

Copyright © 2018 Great Commandment Network

ISBN: 978-1-4245-5621-2 (softcover)
ISBN: 978-1-4245-5622-9 (e-book)

Stock or custom editions of BroadStreet Publishing titles may be purchased in bulk for educational, business, ministry, fundraising, or sales promotional use. For information, please e-mail info@broadstreetpublishing.com.

Cover design by Chris Garborg at garborgdesign.com
Interior by Katherine Lloyd at theDESKonline.com

Printed in the United States of America

18 19 20 21 22 5 4 3 2 1

Contents

A Spirit-Empowered Disciple
LOVES THE LORD

A Spirit-Empowered Disciple
LIVES THE WORD

A Spirit-Empowered Disciple
LOVES PEOPLE

A Spirit-Empowered Disciple
LIVES HIS MISSION

Introduction

Parenting is one of the most rewarding relationships God has created. And yet, if we're honest, many of us find that we don't really know what being a father or mother looks like. We've had few role models or experiences that fill in the blanks. The good news is that when it comes to building relationships in our home, our heavenly Father has the blueprints. We may not always know how to parent our children, but He has the plan to guide us. We may not always feel secure in our parenting choices or know how to face the ever-changing challenges of our culture, but we can rest assured because Jesus is our Cornerstone.

In *31 Days of Prayer for My Children*, you'll find challenging, encouraging, and practical steps to call upon the Cornerstone. In guided prayer moments, you'll be invited to have your own encounter with Jesus, where you'll spend time reflecting on how He relates to you, and have an opportunity to respond to Him. These moments will be critical, because encounters with Jesus produce change. For instance, encountering the acceptance of Christ empowers acceptance of our children; encountering the loving initiative of Jesus prompts additional caring initiative in our homes.

In *31 Days of Prayer for My Children,* you'll also have the opportunity to experience the truth of God's Word—times when you will actually *do* Bible verses—rather than just coming to know them or understand them. Doing God's Word first ourselves and then with our children will produce some of the much-desired transformation in our homes.

Finally, we've designed *31 Days of Prayer for My Children* for your enrichment, encouragement, and growth as a person—not only as a parent. As you spend time with Jesus, in His Word and doing His Book, your life will forever be changed.

May God richly bless your time with Jesus and your relationship with your children.

Terri Snead
Executive Editor, Great Commandment Network

The Great Commandment Network is an international collaborative network of strategic kingdom leaders from the faith community, marketplace, education, and caregiving fields who prioritize the powerful simplicity of the words of Jesus to love God, love others, and see others become His followers (see Matthew 22:37–40; 28:19–20).

Day 1

Why Pray for My Children?

Why is it important to dedicate the time or make it a priority to pray for your children? Setting aside thirty-one days to pray for your kids makes sense for many reasons. Here are just a few of them:

- **As we pray** for our children, we're joining Jesus as He prays on their behalf.

Hebrews tells us that Jesus "lives forever to intercede with God on [our] behalf" (Hebrews 7:25). And the book of Romans reminds us that "he is sitting in the place of honor at God's right hand, pleading for us" (Romans 8:34). Don't you imagine the Savior's prayer list includes your children? When you pray, you have the privilege of joining Jesus in prayer for them.

- **As we pray** for our children, we're joining Jesus in His celebrations.

In Christ's last moments on earth, He revealed His loving desire for us: "that My joy may be in you, and that your joy may be made full" (John 15:11 NASB). Jesus finds joy in your children and in your family. Since family is a special representation of Christ's love, He feels a special joy when He sees families thriving. He loves when our relationships are a testimony to a hurting world. When you pray, you have the privilege of joining Jesus in a celebration of the beauty of family (see Psalm 127:3).

- **As we pray** for our children, we're joining Jesus in His concern.

Raising children is hard at times. Jesus feels compassion for the struggles in your family and any challenges you or your children might be facing. His heart is moved with compassion when He sees you or your family hurting, disappointed, discouraged, or alone. So join Jesus in praying for your son or daughter, lifting up concerns and asking the Lord to give you a deeper understanding of your child's heart. Praying for your children allows the Holy Spirit to help you see what He sees so you can love them the way Jesus loves (see 2 Corinthians 1:2–4).

- **As we pray** for our children, we strengthen our own walk with Jesus.

Spending time with our Savior deepens our closeness with Him. As you pray, the Spirit will minister to your heart, to your needs, and to your concerns. Parents, let's pray for our children! Let's pray often. Let's pray consistently. Let's pray boldly. Let's pray faithfully (see Romans 8:26–27).

Take the next few moments and join Jesus in prayer.

* Jesus, when I imagine that I can join you in prayer, my heart feels grateful because _____.

* I want to join you in prayer for my children. First, I'm grateful for my children because _____.

* I lift up my children to you and pray specifically that you would _____.

Day 2

How to Pray
for My Children

This world—where the prince of darkness seeks to steal, kill, and destroy families—needs Christ followers who walk in the light (see John 10:10; 12:35 NASB). For the next thirty-one days, we encourage you to take a journey of walking in the light. During your times of prayer, you will walk in the light of God's Son, God's Word, and God's people (see John 8:12; Matthew 5:14; Psalm 119:105).

As you take this journey, you will spend moments in personal prayer but also pray for your children. You'll pray for your children to:

- encounter Jesus in fresh, new ways,
- live out the Bible frequently, and
- interact with people by demonstrating God's love.

Let's try one of your own fresh encounters with Jesus. As you read these words from the Savior, imagine that He's speaking directly to you. Listen for His compassionate, strong voice. He's thrilled to share these moments with you.

PRAY: LISTEN TO JESUS

The darkness of this world is all around you, and I don't want your family to be overtaken. I have a plan. I have a plan for your protection, guidance, and strength. If you'll spend time with me, my Word, and my people, darkness won't have a chance in your family. As you encounter me, I will protect you, because I'm the Light of the World. Let my Word guide you and light your way. Let my people encourage you and give you strength. Walking in the light is the best place to be because that means we're walking together (see John 8:12; Matthew 5:14; Psalm 119:105).

Now voice your personal prayer to Jesus:

* Jesus, when I look at the darkness of this world, I feel especially concerned about _____.

* Lord, I am grateful for your protection, guidance, and strength, particularly because _____.

* Jesus, I also pray for my children. I pray they would come to know you and spend more time with you, your Word, and your people so darkness doesn't have a chance in our home and in our family.

* I pray you would protect my children from _____.

* I pray you would guide my children in _____.

* I pray you would strengthen my children in _____.

As you continue this journey of prayer, remember the goal: Your times of prayer can't just be focused on training your children.

These moments with Jesus and His Word are designed to first develop Christlikeness within you. The destination of your journey is a person, and His name is Jesus. As you spend time focused on getting to know Christ and experiencing more of His love, and as you spend time focused on living out His Word, not just reading or hearing it, you'll become more like Him. This journey will change something—and hopefully it's you.

You may be thinking: *My children need to change in some areas. Our family needs to be stronger, closer, or different in certain ways. What can I do?*

Here are a few things you can do:

Pray. Have your own encounters with Jesus, and see what changes He might want to make in you.

Live. Consistently live out God's Word and *do* the Bible in your home. Watch His Word make a difference in your life and in the lives of your children.

Act. Use the ideas from this resource and take practical action steps. Take initiative to love your children in practical, relevant ways.

Pray, live, and act. Then watch the power of God's Son, His Word, and His people make a difference in your children and in your family.

Day 3

What to Pray
for My Children

This book is designed to foster a Spirit-empowered faith—a faith that is demonstrable, observable, and only possible with the empowerment of the Holy Spirit. A framework for this kind of spiritual growth has been drawn from a cluster analysis of several Greek and Hebrew words that declare that Christ's followers are to be equipped for works of service (see Ephesians 4:12). Therefore, in *31 Days of Prayer for My Children*, you'll find specific sections that are designed around four themes (see Appendix 3, page 125). A Spirit-empowered disciple

- **Loves the Lord** (see Luke 10:38–42). You will find seven days of prayer marked L1, L2, L3, L4, L7, L8, and L10.

- **Lives the Word** (see 2 Corinthians 3:2). You will find seven days of prayer marked W2.

- **Loves People** (see Ephesians 4:29). You will find seven days of prayer marked P3.

- **Lives His Mission** (see 1 Thessalonians 2:8). You will find seven days of prayer marked M1.

Our world needs families who live as Spirit-empowered disciples who are making disciples who, in turn, make disciples. Thus, *31 Days of Prayer for My Children* rightly focuses on the powerful simplicity of

- loving God,
- living His Word,
- loving people, and
- living His mission.

After three days of prayer focused on why, how, and what to pray for your children, we will turn our attention to specific prayer themes. Before we focus on these thematic prayers, however, we invite you to live out God's Word. God tells us that if we ask anything according to His will, He hears us and grants our request (see 1 John 5:14–15). We know it's His will for us to love our children well, so we can count on Him to grant this request.

Spend the next few moments in prayer. Make your request to God and look for how He gives to you. Jesus said, "If you ask the Father for anything in My name, He will give it to you" (John 16:23 NASB).

LIVE: DO THE BIBLE

God, I know it's your will for me to love my children well, so I'm asking you to give me whatever I need to love the way you want me to love. If I need to change, show me. If I need to see things differently, I'm ready. I'm asking these things in your name, knowing that you'll answer my prayer and give me what I ask for. In Jesus' name, amen.

A Spirit-Empowered Disciple
LOVES THE LORD

Day 4

Closer to Him

May we talk to and listen to God in prayer for our daily decisions and direction for life as a demonstration of our love for Him.

STORIES FROM A PARENT'S HEART

I struggled throughout my life with overwork. My wife and I argued about family priorities often; we were definitely in agreement about this challenge. My wife told me that I was way too preoccupied with things at the office. I tried to change, even shedding tears on many occasions over my compulsion to work and my tendency to neglect our family.

This dilemma of parenting led us to a counselor's office. One day, with tears streaming down my cheeks, I shared, "You know, I think a major reason why I don't go home is that I'm afraid. I'm afraid that I don't know how to be a father. I know my children need me, but I'm not sure I know how to give to them. I feel adequate at work, but I don't feel adequate with my own children."

I've also discovered that I'm not alone in this struggle. Many parents—fathers and mothers alike—feel inadequate with their own children. Parenting isn't easy. Raising spiritually, emotionally, and physically healthy children can be incredibly challenging at times. That's why our first goal as a parent is to become a disciple—a learner, one who is taught, one who listens to and follows Jesus.

PRAY: LISTEN TO JESUS

I long to have quiet moments of conversation with you. I love when you are still and free of distractions, because those are the times when you can truly feel my love. I have equipped you with everything you need, so come to me often and I'll remind you of my gifts. I especially enjoy seeing you pray together as a family. When all of us come together in prayer, miraculous things can happen. Remember, I am the God of love. So it's in these quiet moments of time with me that I can be your unlimited source of sacrificial love (see Psalm 46:10; 2 Timothy 3:17; 1 John 4:8).

* Jesus, I ask that you quiet my mind and my spirit. Help me to focus on you. In my relationship with my kids, I am depending upon you to _____. Sometimes I don't know how to _____, so I'm counting on you to teach me _____.

* Lord, since you are the God of love, I am counting on you to _____. I ask that you empower me to love my children by _____.

LIVE: DO THE BIBLE

Are any of you suffering hardships? You should pray.

—JAMES 5:13

* God, I come to you now about the challenges we are facing. I need to know that you care about _____. Please
reassure me of your love. I need you to intervene in this
situation and empower and equip me to _____.

* God, I pray for my children. They need to know that you
care about these challenges. Please reassure them of
your love. They need you to intervene and equip in this
situation because _____.

TAKE ACTION

* Invite your children to pray with you about any decisions
they may be facing. Ask God to give you both clear direction and certainty.

* Invite your children to pray with you about any struggles
or hardships they may be facing. Ask the Lord for wisdom and guidance. Let your children hear you call upon
the heavenly Father and voice your trust in His care. Look
for how God answers, and then be sure to celebrate His
provision.

CLAIM HIS PROMISES

Come near to God and he will come near to you.

—JAMES 4:8 NIV

Love the Lord L-2:
A Spirit-empowered disciple listens to and hears God for daily
decisions and direction for life.

Day 5

Living Out
Our Identity

May we come to live joyfully and confidently in our identity as one who is loved by God and belongs to Him.

STORIES FROM A PARENT'S HEART

I've discovered that no single factor is more closely associated with successful growing up than one's sense of identity: *Who am I?* Identity is sometimes thought of as one's internalized picture of oneself. Thus, people can like, dislike, or even hate themselves. This is just one reason why shaping a child's sense of identity is of major importance in the parenting journey.

We all have an eternal significance to our Creator; we have a special identity to Him. As a parent, I have the privilege for a few short years to affirm the identity that the Father has declared in my children. Here's what God says is true about my children: God has declared them worth the gift of His Son. God says that His deepest desire is that my children belong to His family—as joint-heirs with Jesus. God says that as my children come to follow Jesus, they are blessed with every spiritual blessing and can do all things through Christ (see Romans 6:23; 8:16–17; Ephesians 1:3; Philippians 4:13).

As our children come to embrace their incalculable worth to the heavenly Father, find security in their belonging as joint heirs with Christ, and experience the competency of every spiritual blessing, they will enter adult life prepared and motivated to lead the life that God intends.

PRAY: LISTEN TO JESUS

You are a treasure. My Father has declared that you are worth the gift of His Son. You are one of the majestic ones in whom I delight. Remember, dear one: You belong to a royal family. You are a joint heir in my kingdom; you belong to me, as I belong to my Father. Since you are a member of our family, you have been blessed with every spiritual blessing. You can do everything that you need to do as you find your strength in me. Children are gifts from me. Gifts are to be treasured, valued, studied, protected, and cherished (see Psalms 16:3; 127:3; Romans 6:23; 8:16–17; Philippians 4:13; 1 Corinthians 3:23).

* Jesus, I feel _____ when I hear your declaration of my worth, belonging, and how you have equipped me with every spiritual blessing. I'm especially grateful for _____.

* Lord, how do I need to treasure my children? Show me how I can cherish and value the precious gifts you have given me. Guide me in how to affirm their identity, so they _____.

LIVE: DO THE BIBLE

Every single moment you are thinking of me! How precious and wonderful to consider, that you cherish me constantly in your every thought!

—Psalm 139:17 TPT

* God, as I consider that you are thinking of me every single moment and that I am constantly in your thoughts, I am filled with gratitude because _____.

* God, in the same way, I want my children to consider and experience the wonder of how you cherish them. Help me to convey that truth in meaningful ways by _____.

TAKE ACTION

• Affirm your children's *worth* by doing things they like to do and by talking about their dreams, goals, ideas, feelings, and opinions. Accept your children's differences with patience and care.

• Affirm your children's *belonging* with plenty of verbalized love: "I've been thinking today about what a gift you are to our family and how much I love you."

• Affirm your children's *competence* by encouraging them to try new skills. Look for ways to support and build their confidence. Set goals with your children and celebrate when they are accomplished.

CLAIM HIS PROMISES

> *It is through him that we live and function and have our identity; just as your own poets have said, "Our lineage comes from him."*
>
> —ACTS 17:28 TPT

Love the Lord L-4:
A Spirit-empowered disciple lives joyfully and confidently in their identity as one who is loved by God and belongs to Him.

Day 6

An Attitude of Gratitude

May we cultivate a spirit of gratitude and thanksgiving as a demonstration of our love for the Lord.

STORIES FROM A PARENT'S HEART

Wonder and awe must have been at least part of what Mary felt when she made her joyful declaration to God: "My soul magnifies the Lord" (Luke 1:46 ESV). Mary's exaltation and gratitude were not about possessions, position, or status, but about relationship. As the most blessed of all women, Mary's blessing came through a divinely provided relationship. Her exaltation and worship were responses to gifts from the Father.

In a similar way, those of us who have children have been divinely blessed with gifts from the Lord (see Psalm 127:3). The apostle James also reminds us that every good and perfect gift comes down from the Father above (see James 1:17). The same God who blessed Mary with His announcement of Christ has given us some of His most special gifts.

They are the good (and sometimes perfect) gifts my God has given me. Because of this, my soul magnifies the Lord.

PRAY: LISTEN TO JESUS

In case you're unsure of how to connect with me, I've given you a hint: Thank me. I've given you everything you enjoy— every breath you breathe and every relationship you call dear. It's my absolute joy to give, yet it hurts my heart when the ones I love forget to say thank you. I feel loved and honored when I hear your words of gratitude. My followers who have learned to acclaim me walk in my presence and find great blessing. Your gratitude keeps us close (see Psalms 50:23; 69:30; 89:15; 1 Thessalonians 5:18).

＊ Jesus, I don't ever want you to feel disappointed because I forget to say thank you. When I imagine how much you have given to me and our family and how you might experience hurt because of my lack of gratitude, I feel _____.

＊ Lord, I don't want to forget to say thank you for my children. Remind me of all the ways my children are a special blessing from you. Keep me from being critical, negative, or harsh. I'm grateful you have given them to me because _____.

LIVE: DO THE BIBLE

Then I will praise God's name with singing, and I will honor him with thanksgiving.

—Psalm 69:30

* God, I want to bring you honor with my gratitude. Remind me of some of the special ways you have recently loved me. Today, I am particularly grateful for these ten things: _____.

* God, in the same way, I pray for my children. Would you move my children's hearts with gratefulness for how you have loved and cared for us? I want them to feel especially thankful for _____.

TAKE ACTION

• Share a post on social media or find some other public way to demonstrate your gratitude for your children: "I've recently been reminded of some of the great qualities in my children. I don't say it enough: I'm grateful God gave them to me because _____."

• Begin each day by modeling gratitude with and for your child: "I woke up this morning so grateful that God has loved us by _____. What are you glad about?" (See Psalm 90:14.)

CLAIM HIS PROMISES

But giving thanks is a sacrifice that truly honors me. If you keep to my path, I will reveal to you the salvation of God.

—Psalm 50:23

Love the Lord L-1:
A Spirit-empowered disciple consistently practices thanksgiving and gratitude for all things and in all circumstances.

Day 7

Be a Bethany

May we demonstrate our love for the Lord with a lifestyle of worship of Him.

STORIES FROM A PARENT'S HEART

Bethany was a small town, two miles outside of Jerusalem. The city was the home of three of Christ's friends—Mary, Martha, and Lazarus. Aside from that fact, the town was pretty insignificant. Bethany didn't have great historical, political, or even religious importance, but Jesus seemed to go out of His way to get there. I wonder why?

Bethany was a place of refuge for Jesus. It was a place where people He loved wanted to share moments of worship with Him. Bethany was the place where Mary chose to sit at Jesus' feet and hear the vulnerable places of His heart. Jesus must have loved being in Bethany because it was a place where He could both give and receive love (see Luke 10:38–42).

Jesus has this same desire for His relationship with you. Christ longs for you and your family to be His Bethany; He longs for you to be the place where He can give and receive love.

PRAY: LISTEN TO JESUS

Dear one, I am hoping that you will be my Bethany. I am hoping to have a special, one-of-a-kind friendship with you. I want to share my joy with you. I want to share the things that have saddened my heart with you. Just like in Bethany, I want to lavishly give and receive love from you. I am ready to share closeness and vulnerable moments just with you (see Proverbs 3:32).

*   Jesus, I am amazed that you desire for me to be your Bethany. I am grateful when I consider that you want this kind of relationship with me because _____.

*   Lord, I want to share moments of worship with you and for you because _____. You are deserving of my praise because _____.

LIVE: DO THE BIBLE

Worship the LORD with reverence and rejoice with trembling.

—PSALM 2:11 NASB

*   God, I declare my devotion to you because you are

    _____.

*   Lord, I rejoice in my ability to share life and a loving relationship with you because _____. I also want to rejoice with trembling awe. You alone, are great because

    _____.

TAKE ACTION

- Share spiritual conversations with your child. Talk about the greatness of our God. Tell your children about His wonderful deeds and praise Him aloud so your children can hear. Together, rejoice in Him.

- Attend corporate worship services with your children. Remind them that singing praise songs is one way to worship the Lord and tell others how great He is!

- Start a book of blessings, where you ask the Lord to remind you of the great things He has done for you and your family. Record them in the book. Reminisce about these blessings, then pray and worship together as a family.

CLAIM HIS PROMISES

"A time is coming and has now come when the true worshipers will worship the Father in the Spirit and in truth, for they are the kind of worshipers the Father seeks. God is spirit, and his worshipers must worship in the Spirit and in truth."

—JOHN 4:23–24 NIV

Love the Lord L-7:
A Spirit-empowered disciple enjoys a lifestyle of worshiping the Lord—with both private and public expressions of worship.

Day 8

A Student of My Child

May we demonstrate our love for the Lord by imitating Him and living out His kindness for one another.

STORIES FROM A PARENT'S HEART

In families, kindness means discerning the unique needs of a specific person. It involves taking the initiative to express care based on what you know of them. Kindness requires becoming a lifelong "student" of each person in the family—seeking to understand everyone so you can best love them.

The apostle Peter referred to this when he encouraged husbands to "live with your wives in an understanding way" (1 Peter 3:7 NASB). Proverbs encourages a wife to "open her mouth in wisdom and [let] the teaching of kindness [be] on her tongue. She looks well to the ways of her household" (31:26–27 NASB). And Scripture reminds us that *everyone* who has been called by God is to put on a heart of compassion and kindness (see Colos...

I can show Nicholas kindness like no one else... him so well. For example, I buy the brand of T-shi... comfortable in, and I cut his sandwiches in triangle...

25

his favorite shape! I try to prioritize time for Nicholas to play with Caleb, because Nicholas says they are both good at sharing. I know Kara likes to hang out with her friend Chloe, but always at our house, because sometimes the two of them can get into disagreements. I make a special effort to straighten Chloe's covers at night because she can't sleep if they're "all crooked." These demonstrations of kindness are possible because I've learned to be a student of my children. I'm praying that my demonstrations of kindness are just a small way I can imitate the kindness the Lord has shown to me.

PRAY: LISTEN TO JESUS

Remember, my beloved: I am wonderfully kind, patient, and tolerant of you. It was my kindness, in spite of your sin, that first drew you into a relationship with me. Now I'm giving you the opportunity to share some of that kindness with your children. Pay it forward every day. Look for ways to demonstrate kindness with others. Take thought of others just as I think of you a thousand times a day. Finally, remember that sharing truth with one another is important, but that truth needs to be coupled with kindness (see Romans 2:4; Proverbs 3:3; Ephesians 4:15; Psalm 139:17).

* Jesus, you are right—you have been patient, kind, and tolerant of me even though I _____. I am grateful for your kindness toward me because _____. I pray that you would empower me to demonstrate this same kindness with my children. I need your help to _____.

* Lord, I pray that my children would have a fresh experience of your kindness as they live with me. May they sense your patience and understanding and the generous way you love through our daily interactions. I pray specifically that my children would, in turn, show your kindness to _____.

LIVE: DO THE BIBLE

Be kind to each other, tenderhearted, forgiving one another, just as God through Christ has forgiven you.

—EPHESIANS 4:32

* God, remind me often of my children's preferences and uniqueness. Show me what I need to understand about them. Based on these special insights, show me ways I can demonstrate your kindness. Show me ways to be gentle, patient, and accepting. Show me any areas where I need to imitate more of you. Speak to me, Lord. I'm listening.

* Lord, please empower my children to become an imitator of your kindness. Soak my children in more and more of your love so they can have a personal relationship with you and then demonstrate their love for you by _____.

TAKE ACTION

• Look for opportunities to show your children an extra measure of kindness without expecting anything in return. Serve your children's favorite meal or offer to help them clean their rooms. (If that's an unusual gesture of kindness!)

- Talk with your children about how to demonstrate kindness to a friend or neighbor. Bake cookies for the neighbor who's been ill. Rake leaves for the elderly friend down the street. Talk about the kindness of Jesus and how He is pleased when we do the same.

- Compliment your children on their appearance. Encourage compliments of others: "Let's think of a compliment that we can give to _____ today!"

CLAIM HIS PROMISES

Those who are kind benefit themselves, but the cruel bring ruin on themselves.

—Proverbs 11:17 NIV

Love the Lord L-10:
A Spirit-empowered disciple becomes more and more like Jesus by imitating Him and enjoying consistent times of being in His presence.

Day 9

Baseball and Boldness

May we demonstrate our love for God by talking to Him consistently, praying with boldness and trusting Him to answer.

STORIES FROM A PARENT'S HEART

It started out as a "good experience" and an opportunity to play with a team that matched our son's athletic ability. But the baseball season ended with angry coaches and stressed-out kids. Needless to say, my husband and I were relieved when the last game rolled around.

Wayne and I had been praying together for weeks, asking God to show us how to navigate the stressful situations and conflicted relationships. We prayed for God to get us through without losing our tempers. On that last Saturday morning, we finally decided to include our son, Jonathan, in our final conversation and prayer. We talked about how this season had been good at times and hard at times. We talked about how Jonathan had learned a lot about baseball and made some new friends. Then out of a little guilt and desperation, we asked Jon to pray with us.

In his matter-of-fact eight-year-old voice, our son taught us a huge lesson in prayer. Here's what he said: "God, I know you can answer my prayer. I just hope you help us have a good game today. I want to play good, but I really want you to help me and my team have fun. Amen." It was a simple, bold, and faith-filled prayer.

God answered Jon's prayer in more ways than we could have imagined that day. The team won the game we were "supposed" to lose. Coaches relaxed and helped the boys play hard but have fun. And Jonathan hit his first out-of-the park home run. That day began a new discipline of including our kids in times of prayer. That day began a new discipline of praying with boldness and praying with faith.

PRAY: LISTEN TO JESUS

Trust me completely, then look for how I will provide. I am your security; you can count on my faithfulness. My faithfulness is as enduring as the heavens. Your demonstration of faith in me makes my heart sing. There are great blessings in store for the ones who put their faith in me: the faith-filled receive my protection, my favor, and a place of undeserved privilege. Place your faith in me and my Word and watch the things you hope for come into reality (see Philippians 4:19; Proverbs 2:8; 3:26; Psalm 89:2; Matthew 8:10; Romans 5:2; Hebrews 11:1, 6).

* Jesus, I want to please you. So I am declaring my trust in this area of my life: _____. Please show me in your Word how the things I hope for can be turned into demonstrations of faith in you (see Romans 15:4).

❋ Lord, I also pray that my children would come to believe in you and the power of prayer. I pray my children would feel your blessing as they trust in you. Help my children see that you can answer prayer, especially about _____.

LIVE: DO THE BIBLE

Faith shows the reality of what we hope for; it is the evidence of things we cannot see.

—Hebrews 11:1

❋ God, as I consider my relationship with my child, I am hoping for _____. And because I know that my faith pleases you, I am counting on you to _____.

❋ Lord, I ask that you give my children opportunities to see how prayer changes things. I know they are hoping for _____. Please reveal how we might demonstrate more faith in you so we can please you.

TAKE ACTION

• Ask your children to join you in prayer, trusting God to meet a specific need. Talk about how God meets our needs (He doesn't necessarily provide everything we want). God is also in charge of the timing and details of how He provides. Once you're sure that your child's request is truly a need, pray boldly. Pray out loud together, and then watch for God's answer to prayer.

- Memorize specific Bible promises that are you longing
  to see happen, and pray those together with your child.

CLAIM HIS PROMISES

*If you have faith the size of a mustard seed, you will tell this
mountain, "Move from here to there," and it will move. Nothing will be impossible for you.*

—Matthew 17:20 HCSB

Love the Lord L-8:
A Spirit-empowered disciple demonstrates a consistent, bold,
and believing prayer life.

Day 10

Seeing God
as He Really Is

May we deepen our love for the Lord by developing a correct view of Him and enjoying more and more closeness with Him.

STORIES FROM A PARENT'S HEART

What kind of God do you have? We all have different perceptions of God's character and a slightly different view of how He relates to us.

Do you have an inspecting God? Is it almost as if He has a heavenly tally sheet and carefully records everything you do? This kind of God inspects your every move and then relates to you according to how many good marks or bad marks have been given.

Do you have a disappointed God? Does He look at you and seem to never like what He sees? He may notice your attempt at living a good life, but ultimately shakes His head in disappointment.

Do you have a distant or uninvolved God? This kind of God is often too busy to notice your small concerns. He hears you and you talk to Him, but He sits behind His big desk and gives only half-hearted attention. He's nice but maybe too distracted with "more important" things.

The real God is much different than these so-called Gods. He's attentive and caring. The real God's care is so deep and so strong that even a mother's love pales in comparison. He thinks of you so often and is so excited about the possibility of relationship with you that He's "tattooed" your name on the palm of His hand (see Isaiah 49:16). He's not inspecting; He's admiring His creation in you. The real God is excited to love you!

PRAY: LISTEN TO JESUS

There's nothing stronger than a parent's love. In fact, I see that love every time our Father looks at you. Remember, our Father is pleased with you, and He knows you by name. He isn't disappointed or angry with you. Our Father isn't busy inspecting you either; His loving-kindness is new every morning. It's also important to remember that our Father isn't distant from you or disinterested in your life. He's with you— He'll never leave you—and He's so attentive that His thoughts about you are too numerous to count.

I also see the joy in your face when you take time to truly see your own children. Children are some of the Father's most precious gifts, so be sure to take the time to unwrap and admire them. Parenting is hard, so let me be your provider and guide. Just ask me for help, for I love to give it to you (see Exodus 33:12; Lamentations 3:23; Hebrews 13:5; Psalms 25:5; 40:5; 127:3; Matthew 7:11).

* Jesus, I want to demonstrate the kind of love you have for me to my children. Remind me often of my Father's love, and then help me live that out in our family. I especially need your help in this area: _____.

* Lord, help me to see the real you. I want to know you more because my kids need _____, so please give me an extra dose of your _____.

LIVE: DO THE BIBLE

Children are a gift from God; they are his reward.

—Psalm 127:3 TLB

* Jesus, please help me to unwrap the gifts you have given me. Slow me down so I can truly know them. What about my children do you want me to admire? What do you want me to see about their needs? Their future? How can I come alongside you and parent our children well?

* Lord, give me divine insight into what my children need to see about you and the way you love us. I pray specifically that my children would know these aspects of your character _____ (forgiveness, attentiveness, grace, patience, being slow to anger, kindness, strength, peace, and self-control).

TAKE ACTION

• Initiate a conversation with your children about the character of God. Talk about the real God and how He isn't like a policeman or scary school principal. He isn't like a disappointed coach or a disinterested spectator. The real God is excited to love you.

- Take some quiet moments to plan and have a conversation with your child—just to get to know them. Do an internet search for creative discussion questions. Unwrap your gift a little more each day.

- Ask your children to draw the expression on God's face when He sees them each day. Draw your own picture, then talk about the results.

CLAIM HIS PROMISES

In the fear of the LORD one has strong confidence, and his children will have a refuge.

—PROVERBS 14:26 ESV

Love the Lord L-3:
A Spirit-empowered disciple develops a correct view of God as the Lord reveals Himself, enjoying more and more closeness with Him.

A Spirit-Empowered
Disciple
LIVES THE
WORD

Day 11

Cheering for One Another

May we love God's Word and live it out by encouraging one another.

STORIES FROM A PARENT'S HEART

I've decided to declare myself a cheerleader for my kids. At least once a week, I make it a point to tell Adam and Elise how much I believe in them. I cheer them on when things are hard at school or when they get weary of the stress of performing in the school band. I write a special note for my son for his big days on the soccer field. I text Elise just to remind her that I love her and I'm praying for her. I show Adam that I believe in him by not taking over when he's doing his homework or telling him how to do a job around the house. And I make a special effort to speak confidently about my daughter's abilities in front of her friends.

Encouragement isn't just for hard times; it's not just something to give as a last resort. Encouragement is continued gratitude for your child. It means I share hope about my children's future or how they will accomplish their dreams. I say words such as, "Elise,

I'm amazed at how responsible you are. You get your science done without any help from me. I know you want to be a pediatrician someday. You're well on your way!" Encouragement also means that I share words of excitement about their future: "Adam, God has given you a special gift with younger children. You're going to be an awesome dad one day!"

PRAY: LISTEN TO JESUS

Come to me when you are discouraged or weary. Come closer to me when life is hard. I can give you rest. While you are in this world, there will be trouble, but take heart, I have overcome the troubles of this world. Remember that I can fill you with joy and peace in the midst of hard times. I am able to give you sufficiency and abundance for everything I have called you to do (see Matthew 11:28; Romans 15:13; 2 Corinthians 9:8; John 16:33).

* Jesus, thank you for being my encourager. I am weary at times, in _____, and I need your _____. Sometimes it's hard to keep going in _____, so I need your _____.

* Lord, I also pray that you would lift up and encourage my children. Give them strength in _____. Bring other people into my children's lives who will come alongside and cheer them on as _____.

LIVE: DO THE BIBLE

So encourage each other and build each other up, just as you are already doing.

—1 THESSALONIANS 5:11

＊ God, show me the areas where my children might be weary or need someone to cheer them on. Show me the ways in which it might be hard for my children to keep going. Help me to know exactly what encouragement is needed and how to communicate it. Speak to my heart, for I am listening.

＊ Jesus, it seems as if it's hard for them to keep going in the area of _____. Help me build up and show I believe in them. Help me communicate my encouragement in ways that are meaningful.

＊ God, help me create an environment where my children feel encouraged so they can then give it to others. Empower my children to give to _____.

TAKE ACTION

• Send your child a note that begins with these words: "I know it's hard sometimes. I want you to know that I believe in you and your _____" or, "I think you are an amazing kid! I believe in you and I know you can _____."

• Ask your child: "I know _____ can be tough, so how can I encourage you? What words would you like to hear when you get tired, overwhelmed, or frustrated?"

• Surprise your child with a favorite breakfast in bed. Say, "It's going to be a great day, because I have confidence in you and how you're going to _____!"

- Give a small gift along with a pun that makes your child smile (for example, a paper fan with a note that reads, "I'm your biggest fan!").

- If your child has a test or a tough game ahead, write a note on the car window that says, "A hardworking kid sits here!" or, "You've got this!"

CLAIM HIS PROMISES

And God is able to make all grace abound to you, so that always having all sufficiency in everything, you may have an abundance for every good deed.

—2 CORINTHIANS 9:8 NASB

Live the Word W-2:
A Spirit-empowered disciple lives the Word by demonstrating a love for God's Word and living it out every day.

Day 12

A Divine Commodity

May we love God's Word and live it out, especially as we accept one another.

STORIES FROM A PARENT'S HEART

My son is so different from me. I am laid back, while he's high-energy and strong-willed. I'm flexible, while he's a perfectionist. I'm quiet and reserved, while he's outgoing and likes lots of attention. When my life gets stressful, these differences can make him seem—from my perspective—demanding, loud, and out of control. Those character traits are difficult for me to accept at times.

I have learned that acceptance doesn't necessarily mean condoning a child's behavior; rather, it means looking deeper than someone's actions to see that person's true worth, just as God does with me. Jesus met my ultimate need for acceptance in that while I was still a sinner, He died for me (see Romans 5:8). He looked beyond my faults and saw and met my needs. God's love for me is unmerited (I don't deserve it and can't earn it). It is unconditional (it's not based on what I do or don't do). God's acceptance of me is unlimited (it will never run out or be detained).

When I remind myself of how Christ accepts me, it empowers me to patiently parent my very "different" child.

PRAY: LISTEN TO JESUS

Acceptance is a divine commodity. It's only available from me. You must receive it before you can give it. When my Father allowed me to die in your place, He made a deliberate choice to look beyond your imperfections, inadequacies, and sin to accept you as you are. He also loves you so much that His Spirit won't leave you as you are. His unconditional acceptance is permanent. There is nothing you can do to earn it or lose it. Now I see you as one who is favored, righteous, and worth my blessings (see Romans 5:8; Psalm 5:12; Numbers 6:24–26; Romans 15:7).

* Jesus, you loved me and died for me in spite of my _____. I am filled with gratitude for how you have looked beyond my _____. You see me as one who is favored and righteous even though I _____. Help me accept my children as they are, focusing instead on the changes you desire to make in me.

* Lord, I pray you would help me create a home where my children are reassured of unconditional acceptance. Help me live in such a way that they see how love is not based on _____ or _____. Speak to my children's hearts about how you see them as favored, righteous, and worthy of your blessings. Let my children experience a fresh taste of your acceptance delivered through me.

LIVE: DO THE BIBLE

Therefore, accept each other just as Christ has accepted you so that God will be given glory.

—ROMANS 15:7

* God, I want to accept my children the way you have accepted me. Show me how you see them. I can sometimes only see our differences, disagreements, irritations, idiosyncrasies, or needs for improvement. Help me look beyond _____ and see my children with your eyes and respond with your love.

* Jesus, in the same way, I pray that, while I show acceptance, I would have the wisdom to guide my children's behavior and attitudes. Help them sense more of your acceptance and then empower _____ to accept others, especially _____.

TAKE ACTION

* Try this conversation, keeping it lighthearted and celebrate your differences: "I've noticed that you and I are different in these ways: _____. God made us both special and unique!"

* Write a note to your child that says, "I'm grateful that you are your own unique creation. I love how you _____."

* If one of your children's imperfections shows up, respond with, "We've all got some growing to do, don't we? Remember, I love all of you!"

- Quickly forgive your children when they offend you. Don't pout, reject, or ignore them as punishment.

- Give your children the freedom to express their individuality, preferences, and style—without feeling judged or condemned.

CLAIM HIS PROMISES

My grace is sufficient for you, for power is perfected in weakness.

—2 Corinthians 12:9 HCSB

 Live the Word W-2:
A Spirit-empowered disciple lives the Word by demonstrating a love for God's Word and living it out every day.

Day 13

Tears of Comfort

> May we love God's Word and live it out as we comfort one another.

STORIES FROM A PARENT'S HEART

Jesus ministered comfort throughout His ministry on earth. He often identified with the hurts of others to the degree that He wept with them in their pain (see John 11:35; Luke 19:41). God is the God of all comfort, and the Holy Spirit is often referred to as the Comforter (see 2 Corinthians 1:3; John 14:16). To give comfort means to give strength and hope, to ease the grief or pain of another, to console, and to mourn with those who are mourning.

It's important to learn to recognize times when your children have an increased need for comfort. Watch for times when your children might have experienced rejection or disappointment; when they are physically ill or under stress; when a tragedy has occurred; or when they have gone through a time of loss.

When your children need comfort, refrain from correction ("The reason that happened is …"), teaching ("Next time …"), giving a pep talk ("Come on, it's a beautiful day outside!"), or giving advice ("If you would just …"). Instead, learn to identify with the feelings of your children and then hurt with them. Comfort is an emotional need and is only met with an emotional response.

Finally, in order to give comfort, you'll want to develop your compassion vocabulary. It will include phrases like

- "I'm so sorry that you're hurting."
- "I hurt for you."
- "I'm here for you."
- "I feel compassion for you because _____."
- "It hurts my heart to hear you say _____."

These phrases can be communicated verbally or in writing.

PRAY: LISTEN TO JESUS

Just as I was moved with compassion for my Son, I hurt deeply when I see your sadness, disappointment, and hurt. I will never, ever leave you comfortless. My love, comfort, hope, strength, and grace are always available for you. I am the God of all comfort, so when you're called upon to give compassion to another, call on me (see John 11:1–34; 14:18; 2 Corinthians 1:3–4).

* Jesus, when I imagine that the Savior of the universe hurts for me, cries for me, and is moved with compassion for me, I feel _____. As I receive your care and comfort, let my heart be moved with compassion for others.

* Lord, I also pray that you would give me your words of comfort. I know there are friends and family who have felt _____ about _____ and need some of your comfort. When I reflect on the pain each person is going through, I feel _____ for them.

LIVE: DO THE BIBLE

Weep with those who weep.

—ROMANS 12:15 NASB

* God, I know that my children sometimes feel hurt, sad, or disappointed about _____. Because I love them, it makes me sad to know that my children have gone through this. When I reflect what my children have experienced and what they feel, my heart is moved with compassion because _____.

* In times past, I know they have felt hurt about _____ and likely need some of your comfort. Jesus, help me give comfort to my children. Help me share words like _____.

* Lord, help me create an environment of comfort for my family so my children are equipped to care and comfort others, especially in these ways: _____.

TAKE ACTION

• If your child voices sadness, hurt, or any painful emotion, first sit quietly and listen attentively. Don't try to change, fix, or give advice about the situation.

• Then share words of comfort:
  ○ "Sweetheart, I know you might feel _____, and I want you to know that I'm so sorry you're going through this."
  ○ "It makes me sad to hear you say _____, because I love

you. It hurts my heart to see you hurting."

- ◦ "Thank you for telling me about that. I'm sad that happened."

- • Finally, give your child a hug or a touch on the shoulder, or just sit quietly together.

CLAIM HIS PROMISES

"Show mercy and compassion for others, just as your heavenly Father overflows with mercy and compassion for all."

—LUKE 6:36 TPT

Live the Word W-2:
A Spirit-empowered disciple lives the Word by demonstrating a love for God's Word and living it out every day.

Day 14

It's Good
for the Soul

May we love God's Word and live it out, especially as we confess our sins to one another.

STORIES FROM A PARENT'S HEART

In our family, we hurt each other. We don't mean to, but we do. Unfortunately, those hurts don't simply go away on their own. Time doesn't spontaneously heal resentments. We need to confess the sin behind the hurt and ask each other for forgiveness.

It's sobering to realize that my impatience, my unloving attitude, and my harsh words are the kinds of sin that sent Christ to the cross. Experiencing His redemption and forgiveness frees me to confess my sins and ask Him to forgive me.

As God challenges me to look at how I've hurt others (my children included) and to grieve my hurtful actions, He also promises that He has forgiven me, and it is safe for me to confess my sin to the people I love most. It's still hard for me to say to my child, "Marisa, I know that my words hurt your feelings. I was wrong.

Please forgive me." But I know it is the first step to the freedom of forgiveness. When my daughter says back to me, "Thank you, Mom. I forgive you," I feel cleansed.

I encourage you to practice confession and forgiveness with your kids. First, take time alone to list ways in which you may have hurt your children. Ask yourself, "Have I been selfish, critical, negative, insensitive, disrespectful, verbally abusive, or not attentive?" Then take your list and confess each item to God, then receive His forgiveness and then your children's. Finally, when those inevitable family conflicts occur, encourage your children to share confessions with one another. Experience the freedom of forgiveness.

PRAY: LISTEN TO JESUS

Confession is hard, but it has great reward. Your confession— admitting your wrong actions, attitudes, and behaviors— keeps us in right relationship with one another. You have less worry, guilt, and anxiety when you practice confession with me. When you admit your sin, you can count on my forgiveness. It's a promise. Confessing to another person brings the promise of healing in that relationship too (see 1 John 1:9; Psalms 38:18; 51:1–9; James 5:16; Lamentations 3:23).

* God, I am grateful for your promise of forgiveness and how that keeps me close to you because _____. Thank you that I can empty my guilt, worry, and anxiety through confession. I'm grateful for your loving-kindness because _____.

* Lord, I pray that you would empower me to share any needed confessions with my children. Overwhelm me

with the truth that I can trust your loving-kindness to be new every morning. Please give me the words as I make things right with my children. Help me leave out any justification of my wrong.

LIVE: DO THE BIBLE

I acknowledged my sin to You, and my iniquity I have not hidden.

—Psalm 32:5 NKJV

* God, search my heart and tell me if there are attitudes, behaviors, or habits (especially those that impact my child) that are wrong in your sight and need my confession. Lord, I admit that I was wrong in _____. Will you forgive me for _____? Help me share these points of confession with my children.

* God, I pray for my children. Empower them to receive my confession and forgive me of the sin I have committed. Bring more healing and restoration to our family, especially in the area of _____.

TAKE ACTION

• As needed, set aside a private time with each child. Share the areas of confession that the Lord has revealed to you.

• Avoid excuses or defensiveness in your confession. A great confession sounds like:
  ◦ "I was wrong when _____."
  ◦ "I know you must have felt _____."

○ "Will you forgive me?"

- After you have successfully modeled these principles of confession with your children, when conflicts occur, encourage them to do the same. Remind them they are living out James 5:16.

CLAIM HIS PROMISES

Confess your sins to each other and pray for each other so that you may be healed.

—JAMES 5:16

Live the Word W-2:
A Spirit-empowered disciple lives the Word by demonstrating a love for God's Word and living it out every day.

Day 15

Release Your Grip

May we love God's Word and live it out, especially as we forgive one another.

STORIES FROM A PARENT'S HEART

In Greek, the word for *forgiveness* means "to release." Before, when I forgave, I released the person and the action but failed to release my pain. I forgave, but I still felt hurt later. I wasn't dealing with the pain associated with the hurt.

It's been difficult, but I've discovered that I need to share my pain with the Lord. It's not enough just to "gut it out" and forgive my offender. The Lord wants to heal the hurt that I've endured, and that requires I share it with Him. Jesus wants me to tell Him about my disappointment and let Him comfort me. He wants me to talk with Him about my rejection so He can remind me He understands how deeply I hurt.

One important step in my experience of forgiveness is to imagine myself alone in the garden of Gethsemane with Jesus. I "listen" as He shares His hurt and pain with the Father (see Matthew 26:36–39). Jesus shared His hurt with God, so it must be okay for me to do the same. I imagine the scene of the angels comforting our suffering Savior (see Luke 22:43–44). I'm then free to tell the Father about my own painful experiences and then wait until the God of all comfort pours His healing compassion over me. Finally, I reflect on how Jesus experienced this time of healing and comfort with the Father before He could offer forgiveness at the cross. In the same way, it is my experience of God's compassion and care first that allows me to truly forgive.

PRAY: LISTEN TO JESUS

I am so saddened when you experience hurt. I notice your pain and I hear your cries. Your painful experiences move my heart with compassion. If someone has hurt you, I want to comfort you and help you forgive. I am full of unfailing love for anyone who asks for my help. Make allowances for the faults of others. Forgive them and you will be forgiven. I know releasing is hard, but it's a matter of stewardship. My Father has granted you forgiveness, so now it's your turn to share His gift of forgiveness with others. Remember: If you refuse to forgive, your Father will not forgive you (see Matthew 6:15; Psalm 86:5; Luke 6:31–36; Colossians 3:13).

* Jesus, I need your comfort about my hurt caused by _____. Help me to completely release my pain about _____. Please bring more of your freedom and forgiveness to my life.

* Lord, I pray that you would remind me often that I have done nothing to deserve your forgiveness. I am so grateful for your forgiveness and how your unconditional love

allows me to _____. God, just as you have forgiven me, help me to forgive _____. Help me make allowances for _____. I am trusting the Holy Spirit to _____.

LIVE: DO THE BIBLE

Make allowance for each other's faults, and forgive anyone who offends you. Remember, the Lord forgave you, so you must forgive others.

—COLOSSIANS 3:13

＊ God, help me offer comfort to my children when they are hurt by _____. I want to be your voice of compassion. Guide me in how to lead my children to forgive _____.

＊ Jesus, I pray that you would help me lead our family in the area of forgiveness by _____. Help us make allowances for _____.

TAKE ACTION

• Write a letter to Jesus, telling Him about the hurts you've experienced and any areas of unforgiveness you are stilling clinging to. Allow the Holy Spirit to bring you comfort, healing, and forgiveness for each moment of pain.

• After you have received comfort from the Lord and have a forgiving heart toward your offender, it *may* be time to share your hurt. (Consult with a mentor, counselor, or pastor before sharing with your offender.) That might sound like: "I need to share something that's been hard for me. I care about our relationship and want you to know that it was hurtful when _____ (name the incident without judgment). I felt _____ (name your hurt, not just the anger). Thank you for listening." Then leave the topic, trusting the Holy Spirit to bring healing, confession, and change.

CLAIM HIS PROMISES

Love prospers when a fault is forgiven, but dwelling on it separates close friends.

—PROVERBS 17:9

Live the Word W-2:
A Spirit-empowered disciple lives the Word by demonstrating a love for God's Word and living it out every day.

Day 16

Build Up

> May we love God's Word and live it out, especially as we speak only words that edify one another.

STORIES FROM A PARENT'S HEART

I have worked diligently to model what it means to treat others the way I want to be treated—especially in how I speak to my kids. I try to speak only words that are truthful and kind.

First, I've realized that I must discern the need of the situation before I speak. Ephesians 4:29 tells us that we need to only speak words that fit the need of the moment. It's important that I listen to my child. Is he sad? Then I'll want to show him how much I care. Is she insecure? Then I'll want to reassure her of my love and presence. Is he angry about something? Then I'll want to carefully discern how my gentle answer can turn away his wrath (see Proverbs 15:1).

Second, I try to make sure the timing of my words is right. My child's receptivity to my words is often directly related to the timing of my speaking them. For example, I've learned that it's rarely a good idea to try to land any meaningful training with my kids when they are hungry or right before bedtime. I also have to tailor my words carefully if I need to address my kids' behavior when their friends are around. I don't want to cause feelings of embarrassment or disrespect.

Last, when I need to correct or address behavior, it needs to be done in a way that honors my children and builds them up as God's precious gifts.

PRAY: LISTEN TO JESUS

When I look at you, I celebrate the specialness of you, my creation. Scripture reveals how I'm generous with my edifying words for you. You are my chosen one. You are my masterpiece, the light of the world—holy, blameless, and complete. I want you to have this same view of the people around you. Look for their special qualities and build them up. Think carefully before saying anything that's harsh or unloving. My followers are careful to only speak words that edify those around them (see Proverbs 15:28; Ephesians 1:4; 2:10; Colossians 1:22; Ephesians 4:29).

* God, I'm grateful for your words of edification for me. Thank you for reminding me that you see me as _____. I'm blessed by the truth that you have called me _____.

* Lord, I pray that you would fill my mind with words that are pleasing to you. Remind me how you see my children, and let me only say words that reflect that priority.

LIVE: DO THE BIBLE

Do not let any unwholesome talk come out of your mouths, but only what is helpful for building others up according to their needs, that it may benefit those who listen.

—Ephesians 4:29 NIV

* God, make me generous with praise for my children. What words of edification are most important for them to hear from me? What words of criticism or comparison do I need to get rid of?

* Lord, I pray that my children would live out the command of Ephesians 4:29. Would you help them to say words that are _____ (kind, respectful, truthful).

TAKE ACTION

• After the Lord has reminded you of the positive character traits that are true of your child, share those privately through a text, written note, or verbal affirmation: "I'm so proud that you're my son (daughter) because of your _____." Brag on your child in public settings too.

• Ask your child these questions: "What words would you like to hear from me more often? What words would you like to hear from me less often?"

CLAIM HIS PROMISES

GOD told them, "I've never quit loving you and never will. Expect love, love and more love!"

—JEREMIAH 31:3 MSG

Live the Word W-2:
A Spirit-empowered disciple lives the Word by demonstrating a love for God's Word and living it out every day.

Day 17

Designer Genes

May we love God's Word and live it out, especially as we understand and give preference to one another.

STORIES FROM A PARENT'S HEART

God loves variety. He loves blond hair and blue eyes, brown hair and brown eyes, red hair and green eyes, tall, short, and everything in between. We were each carefully created by the Master Designer, according to His plan—no miscalculations or mistakes. In a sense, we all made our grand entrance into this world wearing designer genes.

These designer genes determine more than just our physical characteristics. Temperament is, for the most part, genetically determined. Some children are hardwired with extremely adaptable temperaments, while for many others change sends them into a tailspin. Some children are wired with predictable rhythms and eat and sleep on a consistent schedule, while other children have little predictability to their eating and sleeping schedules and don't seem to need much routine. A child's activity level, intensity of reaction, and tendency to approach or withdraw from something new are all aspects of a child's temperament that are hardwired by the Master Creator. If you notice a characteristic from birth, that's likely an indication of a child's divine genetic formation.

Here's what I've discovered is important about this "designer genes" perspective. Many times, my child's God-given, hardwired temperament may be completely different from my own or go entirely contrary to my preferences. In order for our home to be the peaceful, loving, and fun environment we all want, I have to

- understand the hardwired temperament of each child;
- accept differences, while lovingly, patiently, and prayerfully guiding behavior; and when possible,
- give preference to the hardwired temperament of my child.

PRAY: LISTEN TO JESUS

Remember, my beloved: I had equal status with my heavenly Father, but I didn't cling to that position. I exchanged my status and the privileges of deity and became human. I did this for you! I gave up myself and gave preference to you and to our relationship. I want this same kind of selflessness to be true of you too. Give preference to one another. Love deeply. Trust in me, and I will lift you up (see Romans 12:10; Philippians 2:1–11; 1 Peter 5:6).

* Jesus, I am grateful for your demonstration of humility and how you gave preference to me because _____. I feel _____ when I imagine that you gave up your position in heaven so you could have a relationship with me.

* Lord, I pray that you would help me to see the ways you have divinely wired my children. In what ways do I need to humbly accept their temperament? Show me any ways in which I need to give preference to my children.

LIVE: DO THE BIBLE

Give preference to one another in honor.

—Romans 12:10 NASB

* God, I want to give preference to my children when it's appropriate. I also want to have the wisdom to address behavior, attitudes, or character in them that are not pleasing to you. Help me to parent my children with patience and love regarding _____.

* Lord, I pray that my children would have this same ability to defer to others. Would you empower them to show preference to one another and selflessly give to others when _____?

TAKE ACTION

• Ask your spouse, parent, or a good friend to help you assess the areas in your child that seem to be divinely wired. Discuss any adjustments that need to be made to accept your child's temperament.

• On age-appropriate topics, ask your children about their preferences—at home, at school, or with friends: "I'd like to know what feels best for you. Would you rather _____ or _____?"

- Ask your older child to share responses to this statement: "In our family, it would mean a lot to me if we could _____."

CLAIM HIS PROMISES

Depend on GOD and keep at it because in the LORD GOD you have a sure thing.

—ISAIAH 26:4 MSG

Live the Word W-2:
A Spirit-empowered disciple lives the Word by demonstrating a love for God's Word and living it out every day.

A Spirit-Empowered
Disciple
LOVES PEOPLE

Day 18

Stamp of Approval

May we share God's love with others, especially as we speak words of approval.

STORIES FROM A PARENT'S HEART

Approval means thinking and speaking well of others. It means commending someone because of who they are, apart from what they do. It means affirming the fact of and importance of a relationship. It's helpful to remember how the Father met the Son's need for approval.

Jesus stood in line with the rest of the followers waiting to be baptized. John the Baptist raised his hand and announced that Jesus of Nazareth was to be baptized that day. As Jesus came out of the water, the heavens opened up and the Spirit of God descended upon Him like a dove. And, out of nowhere, a thundering voice announced, "You are my Son, whom I love; with you I am well pleased" (Mark 1:11 NIV). The Father affirmed both the fact of and the importance of their relationship.

It's also important to notice that the Father initiated this contact. Jesus didn't have to ask for it. And one additional thing to notice is that the Father approved of His Son before the Son had done anything; this blessing came before Jesus had performed any miracles or healed or converted anyone. The Father gave His Son approval because of who He was, not for what He had done.

As the Father approved of the Son, so He approves of you and me. God has also met our ultimate need for approval, affirming us as saints, sons of the Most High, and people for God's own possession (see Romans 1:7; Ephesians 1:5; 1 Peter 2:9).

PRAY: LISTEN TO JESUS

I love you for who you are and apart from what you do. You don't have to do anything to earn my love, and you can't do anything to lose it. I know everything there is to know about you—your strengths and your weaknesses—and still it was the possibility of a relationship with you that brought me to Calvary. You are my beloved; you are chosen. I am pleased with you, and you are one in whom I delight (see Matthew 3:17; Exodus 33:17; Ephesians 1:7; 1 John 3:1).

* Jesus, when I reflect on how you love me apart from what I do, I feel grateful because _____. To consider that you endured Calvary because a relationship with me was important to you, I am moved with feelings of _____.

* Lord, I pray that you would help me experience your approval on a daily basis. Would you give me a fresh experience of your affirming love? Reassure me that you love me apart from what I do or what choices I make.

LIVE: DO THE BIBLE

Commend those who do right.

—1 Peter 2:14 NIV

❋ God, show me some of the ways I can give words of approval and commendation to my children. What character traits should I affirm in them? Show me what you see in my children. I want my children to sense my pride because _____.

❋ God, I pray that my children would see opportunities to affirm, approve, and commend others. Show them positive character traits in others and help them verbalize those traits, especially in these relationships _____.

TAKE ACTION

• Do an internet search for a list of positive character traits. Choose two traits that are true about your child each week. Share them verbally or in writing: "I am so proud you are my son/daughter because you are _____. I see _____ (trait) in you when _____. Out of all the sons/daughters in the world, I would pick you because of your _____."

• Post your child's photo in your office or at home. Put a note in your child's lunch or backpack that says, "You're the apple of my eye!" or "You're the best of the bunch!" or "I'm so glad I get to be your mom/dad!"

• Say these words to your child on a frequent basis: "I love you. Period. There's nothing you can do for me to make me love you more and nothing you can do that will make me love you less."

CLAIM HIS PROMISES

"Give, and it will be given to you."

—LUKE 6:38 NASB

Love People P-3:
A Spirit-empowered disciple loves people by discerning the relational needs of others and sharing God's love in meaningful ways.

Day 19

Hugs and Kisses

May we share God's love in meaningful ways, especially as we give affection to one another.

STORIES FROM A PARENT'S HEART

Affection means expressing care and closeness through appropriate, gentle touch or verbalized love. Demonstrating affection means leaving sweet notes, holding hands, rubbing your child's back, or initiating a late-night tickle session. It looks like giving hugs, kisses, and snuggles on the couch and wrestling for fun. It sounds like: "You're really special. I love you. You mean the world to me! You're God's gift for our family!" It might also include calling your son or daughter just because you wanted to hear their voice. Affection means doing the simple things that show your child that you care.

I've seen this to be true: When we meet our children's need for affection, they often feel more secure and feel free to give to others. As my kids have grown older, it became "uncool" to admit their need for affection. The need was there nonetheless, so I persevered. I gave hugs even when they didn't seem to like it. I still said I love you, but only in private. I want my children to look back and have plenty of memories of my love for them. Don't underestimate the power of your physical connection and verbalized love for your kids.

PRAY: LISTEN TO JESUS

My love for you is an everlasting love; I want you to experience how wide, long, high, and deep my love is for you. Imagine it's evening and you are sitting safely on a boat in the middle of the ocean. The sea is perfectly calm, and the stars are shining brightly. My love is like the horizon. It doesn't end; you just can't see it all at once. My love is higher than the stars; you'll never be able to reach its limits. My love goes on forever; there are no time constraints or expiration dates. My love is deeper than the ocean floor; you'll never reach its end. I love you with an everlasting love (see Isaiah 42:6; Jeremiah 31:3; 1 John 3:1; Ephesians 3:18).

* Jesus, when I imagine that your care for me never ends, my heart is moved with gratitude because _____. When I reflect on your limitless and everlasting love, I am in awe of you because _____.

* Lord, I pray that I would sense the vastness of your love for me. Overwhelm me in new ways with the height, the depth, and the extent of your love, especially as I _____.

LIVE: DO THE BIBLE

"Love each other. Just as I have loved you, you should love each other."

—JOHN 13:34

* God, I want to communicate affection and closeness to my children through my tender words and gentle touch. Help me know the right words to say because _____. Help me to know the right time and meaningful ways to communicate my love, especially as _____.

* Lord, I pray that you would help my children give affection with gentle words and appropriate touch. Help them share more and more of your love by _____.

TAKE ACTION

* Surprise your child by going out of your way to creatively communicate your love. Write a giant note on the driveway or in the backyard that says, "My love for you is as big as _____" or, "You are hugely important to me because _____."

* Pick your child up from school a little early and say, "Hi, sweetheart. I was just thinking about how much I love you and wanted to celebrate. How about some ice cream now and wrestling after dinner?"

* Leave your children in the morning with a smile, a hug, and maybe a kiss. Greet them when you come together

at the end of the day. Welcome your children in a way that lets them know you're *always* glad to see them.

CLAIM HIS PROMISES

No one has seen God, ever. But if we love one another, God dwells deeply within us, and his love becomes complete in us—perfect love!

—1 John 4:12 MSG

Love People P-3:
A Spirit-empowered disciple loves people by discerning the relational needs of others and sharing God's love in meaningful ways.

Day 20

Saying Thanks

May we share God's love in meaningful ways, especially as we give appreciation to one another.

STORIES FROM A PARENT'S HEART

Isn't it a great feeling to be appreciated for something you've done? There is hardly anything like it. We all love to get verbal pats on the back when we do something well. It's part of how we were made. We need others to notice our effort and give us verbal strokes. We need praise that is clear, strong, and accurate so we know beyond a doubt that we are being appreciated. Genuine appreciation is unselfish—an expression of our gratitude for the benefit of another.

One important element in true appreciation is the ability to demonstrate that we see what's right as often as we see what's wrong. If I were to appreciate Gabriel for consistently putting his dishes in the dishwasher, he would know I wasn't sincere. We buy paper plates because the trip from the table to the dishwasher is an often-forgotten journey. I still have to remind my son to clear his plate, so it would not be genuine if I were to praise him for it.

On the other hand, Gabe *would* feel loved if I were to express my gratitude for how he worked hard on his science project or how he took out the trash without complaining. These words of appreciation affirm to Gabriel that I notice what's right as much as I notice what he misses or what is done wrong. Praise your children for the things they do well and the effort they make. Don't let your family come up short in appreciation.

PRAY: LISTEN TO JESUS

I am a God who sees. I see all your steps, I see all that you do and the effort you make, and I intercede on your behalf. You can count on me and my great name; I won't leave you or abandon you in the midst of all you do (see Genesis 16:13; Job 34:21; Romans 8:27).

* Jesus, it makes me feel so grateful to know that you are a God who sees because _____. I am thankful that you notice the things I do and how you intercede for me because _____. I'm grateful I can count on you to be with me in the midst of _____.

* Jesus, remind me often that you see how I _____. Reassure me that you know and acknowledge my effort in _____, even when others miss it.

LIVE: DO THE BIBLE

I thank my God always concerning you.

—1 Corinthians 1:4 NASB

* God, show me what my children do that may often go unnoticed or that I take for granted. Empower me

to take initiative and tell them how much I notice and appreciate what is done well (even if they're not perfect) and the effort that's made. I'm especially grateful today for how my child _____.

✻ Lord, please give my children the special vision to see the things others do and the effort others make. Empower them to speak up and say thank you to others. Help me encourage their thankfulness for _____.

TAKE ACTION

- Appreciate your children in front of their grandparents, siblings, or friends: "I want you to know that my kids are pretty great. They are an amazing help to our family because _____."

- Bring home a special gift, a thoughtfully composed note, or a treat as a demonstration of your appreciation.

- Share these words with your child: "I've noticed some of the things you've done lately, and I want to say thanks for _____."

- Send your children thank-you notes in the mail. Tell them how much you appreciate them.

CLAIM HIS PROMISES

The Lord remembers us and will bless us.

—Psalm 115:12 HCSB

Love People P-3:
A Spirit-empowered disciple loves people by discerning the relational needs of others and sharing God's love in meaningful ways.

Day 21

Undivided Attention

> May we share God's love in meaningful ways, especially as we give attention to one another.

STORIES FROM A PARENT'S HEART

I completed a painful assessment the other day. I asked myself how I was doing at meeting my children's need for attention—more specifically, their need for me to listen. Do I give my kids individual, undivided, and consistent attention?

Individual Attention. Do I purposefully talk and listen to my kids when we are together? Just being in the house together doesn't count. In order to give individual attention, I must actively pursue a specific conversation with both my son and daughter—when I have no agenda other than to know them or more about their world—and be a willing participant in the conversation.

Undivided Attention. Do I make an effort to try to talk with my kids away from any potential interruptions? Do I concentrate on the conversation, or do I daydream, disengage, try to multitask, or look at my phone? Do I dominate the conversation or encourage my kids to talk about their day?

Consistent Attention. Do my children sense my willingness to give plenty of time to discuss difficult subjects, or do I give off signals that I just want them to get to the point? Does listening to my children include a caring heart and loving attitude or lots of advice and criticism? Do my children experience me as regularly available and ready to listen, or am I too often preoccupied or unreliable?

After doing such an assessment, I was sobered by the results. I realized that there were improvements that needed to be made in my life and in our family.

PRAY: LISTEN TO JESUS

I have set my love upon you. I will set you on high, because I know your name. You will call upon me, and I will hear you. I will be with you in trouble; I will deliver you and honor you. Remember, I lean in to listen to the needs of your heart. Cherish the thoughts I have about you—they are precious, rare, and beautiful. I think about you so often that you couldn't even begin to count them. Even if you tried, my thoughts about you would outnumber the sand of the seas (see Psalms 4:3; 91:14–15; 139:17–18).

* Jesus, it amazes me that you lean in and listen to me. I call upon you today and trust that you will hear me about _____. You are attentive to me and my world, and I give you thanks because _____.

* Lord, I pray that I would come to a new understanding of how attentive you are to my needs. Please remind me of your attentiveness and thoughtfulness even when I fail to be attentive to others.

LIVE: DO THE BIBLE

But that the members may have the same care for one another.

—1 Corinthians 12:25 NASB

* God, show me how to give more attention to my children. In what ways do I need to listen to them more effectively and understand them more deeply? What things can we enjoy doing that are part of their world?

* Lord, I pray that my children would become more attentive. Help me teach them how to give undivided attention. I know that I am the model for this, so help me _____ so they are able to _____.

TAKE ACTION

• Say this to your child and be prepared to listen: "Hey, honey, tell me the best part and the hardest part about your day."

• Watch a movie, try a hobby, or go to an event that's purely for your children and appeals to their interests. Talk about why they enjoy the activity, and share how much you enjoy spending time together.

• Say this sentence while making direct eye contact and without distraction: "Tell me about some of the fun things you'd like to do one day (or when you grow up). I'd like to hear them."

CLAIM HIS PROMISES

You faithfully answer our prayers with awesome deeds, O God our savior.

—Psalm 65:5

Love People P-3:

A Spirit-empowered disciple loves people by discerning the relational needs of others and sharing God's love in meaningful ways.

Day 22

Honor and Value

May we share God's love in meaningful ways, especially as we show respect to one another.

STORIES FROM A PARENT'S HEART

Giving respect means valuing and regarding one another highly, treating others as important and honoring one another. The need for respect is not something that magically appears when a person turns twenty-one. We all need to be valued—from day one! Even small children need respect too.

Every child is a unique creation of God. Your children's value is greater than just being the son or daughter of their earthly parents. They're on loan from God, and He has a special plan for each of them. Part of meeting your children's need for respect is recognizing that many of their characteristics are part of their unique design. Children also need to experience respect in at least three distinct areas: their feelings, their opinions, and their possessions. Respect might sound like:

- "I'm listening. Your thoughts and feelings are important to me, and I want to hear them."

- "We'd like to know what you'd like to do on Saturday. We value your input."
- "I understand your need for privacy and your need to have things that belong to you."
- "Javier, you need to ask your brother's permission before you play with his toys."

Respect is never a one-way street, nor is it relinquishing your role as a parent. Respect includes creating an environment where a mom and dad clearly assume their role as parents, while valuing each child's unique design, individual feelings, opinions, and possessions. God intends for each of us to give respect as well as receive it.

PRAY: LISTEN TO JESUS

I place great value on our relationship; in fact, I call you my friend. I chose you and appointed you that you should go and bear fruit and bring honor to my name. Remember that when you call on me, I will rescue you and honor you because I love you. Before honor comes humility, so make sure that you see others as more important than yourself. Give honor to all people (see John 15:15–16; Psalm 91:15; Proverbs 18:12; Philippians 2:3; 1 Peter 2:17).

* Jesus, I feel respected and valued that you would call me your friend because _____. I feel grateful for this honor because _____.

* Lord, I pray that you would remind me often that you have chosen and appointed me. This is a divine honor,

and yet I am humbled because _____. Help me embrace and experience all that this means for me, especially as I _____.

LIVE: DO THE BIBLE

Be devoted to one another in brotherly love. Honor one another above yourselves.

—Romans 12:10 NIV

＊ God, show me new and important ways that I can respect my children. In what ways do I need to defer and let go of my preferences, and in what areas do I need to hold firm? Show me topics that should be open for input, ideas, and feedback. In what ways do I need to think more highly of others than I do of myself? I know my children need my respect in the areas of _____.

＊ Lord, I pray that you would empower my children to give honor to _____. Help my children show respect in the area of _____. Enable them to think more highly of _____ by _____.

TAKE ACTION

• Ask your child, "You have such great ideas. What do you think we should do about _____?" or "Your opinion is really important, so what would you like to do about _____?"

• Arrive on time for events that impact your child. Keep promises. Let go of smaller decisions, tasks, or preferences in favor of the more important goal of a positive relationship with your child. If married, listen to your spouse's perspective about the children and their needs.

- Give choices whenever possible, not edicts: "Would you like to wear your boots or your tennis shoes?" or "What two stuffed animals would you like to give to the toy drive?"

CLAIM HIS PROMISES

The wise are promoted to honor, but fools are promoted to shame!

—Proverbs 3:35 TLB

Love People P-3:
A Spirit-empowered disciple loves people by discerning the relational needs of others and sharing God's love in meaningful ways.

Day 23

Share the Load

May we share God's love in meaningful ways, especially as we support one another.

STORIES FROM A PARENT'S HEART

Giving support means to come alongside and gently help with a problem or a struggle. It means providing appropriate assistance or help to a person in need.

Kids need a partner who will walk alongside them to help navigate the challenges on their path toward maturity. This does not mean completely shouldering the load for them. In the long run, doing so would actually become a hindrance rather than help, because it would convey the message, "This is too hard or too scary for you. You'd better stand aside while I take over." But neither should it mean standing at a distance while your child struggles alone. Rather, offering support involves conveying, both through words and actions, that you are with your child and that you want to assist with the challenges of life, no matter what.

Supporting children can sometimes mean showing them how to tie their shoes, how to change a tire, or how to use the microwave.

Giving support can include helping with homework (without doing it for them), helping with chores (without relieving them of the responsibility), and helping with any task or project that a child deems overwhelming.

God met our ultimate need for support by anticipating the great burden that we could not bear ourselves (the payment for our sins) and by providing the Holy Spirit to equip, comfort, and empower us.

PRAY: LISTEN TO JESUS

I will accomplish what concerns you. My loving-kindness is everlasting, so I will not forsake the works of my hands. I will equip you with everything good, that you may be able to do the things I have called you to do, work which is pleasing in my sight. As you receive my care and my support, be sure to offer support to others. When you carry the burdens of others, you're living out my commands to love others as you have been loved (see Psalm 138:8; Hebrews 13:20–21; Galatians 6:2).

* Jesus, when I read your words and know that you will accomplish what concerns me, I am thankful because _____.

* Lord, to know that you have equipped me with everything I need to do the work you've called me to do, I am incredibly grateful because _____. I am thankful that you have promised not to forsake the work of your hands. What a supportive God you are, because _____.

LIVE: DO THE BIBLE

Carry each other's burdens, and in this way you will fulfill the law of Christ.

—GALATIANS 6:2 NIV

*   God, show me ways that I can help share in my child's burdens. Show me practical ways I can pitch in and bring relief. I could help relieve stress by _____. What life skills does my child need to learn? I need to teach my child how to _____.

*   Lord, help my child to receive support from me and then look for ways to help others. Help my child become more supportive and willing to help by _____.

TAKE ACTION

*   Take initiative to help your children learn a new skill or give your child an opportunity to learn a skill from another adult. Consider their current age and stage of life. What might they need to learn how to do to feel adequate and competent?

*   Say to your children, "I'm willing to work with you and get this done," and "Could I help you with _____? I would like to help in any way I can."

CLAIM HIS PROMISES

"It is more blessed to give than to receive."

—ACTS 20:35

Love People P-3:
A Spirit-empowered disciple loves people by discerning the relational needs of others and sharing God's love in meaningful ways.

Day 24

Home Security

May we discern the relational needs of others and share God's love in meaningful ways, especially as we bring security to our home.

STORIES FROM A PARENT'S HEART

I've discovered that giving security to a child means creating a home environment where there is harmony in relationships. It means creating a home where there is freedom from fear or threat of harm. A secure home is one where adults keep their promises, are dependable, and consistently provide for a child's physical, emotional, and financial needs.

A home that is secure also provides appropriate boundaries for behavior. Although they deny it, my children derive a sense of security from knowing where the limits are and knowing there are parents in their lives who care enough to set rules and actually enforce limits through loving discipline. If I want to effectively teach and train my children, these six things need to be a part of my discipline:

- Intimacy: Knowing my children and letting them know me is the foundation for all effective discipline.

- **Instruction:** My children need me to clearly and briefly explain what is expected of them. I can't just assume they know what to do.
- **Training:** My children often need a model or support in how to do what I have asked.
- **Warning:** My children need me to spell out the clear consequences that will occur if a behavior is not stopped or a task completed.
- **Correction:** My children need for me to follow through and implement the consequences that have been spelled out, with self-control, firmness, and without anger.
- **Reassurance:** After times of correction, my children need moments of reassurance about my love through words, hugs, and other expressions of love.

Appropriate discipline actually meets the need for security. I'm not going to hold my breath waiting for our children to thank me, but I can be confident that I am, indeed, meeting one of their deepest needs.

PRAY: LISTEN TO JESUS

I promise to never leave you or forsake you. I will always meet your needs for food, clothing, and shelter. I will be your ever-present help in times of trouble. You can count on me to be faithful, unchangeable, and constant. I give security for those who trust in me as their Savior. The mountains may be removed, and the hills may shake, but my loving-kindness will not be removed. My promise of peace will not be shaken. I will set you securely on high and protect you fiercely because you have known my name (see Psalms 46:1; 91:14–15; Lamentations 3:23; Hebrews 13:8; John 10:28; Isaiah 54:10).

* Jesus, I'm grateful for your reassurance about _____. I'm thankful for how you have given me security that _____. I am counting on you to _____.

* Lord, I need an extra dose of your reassurance about _____. Remind me often that you are my ever-present help and unchangeable stability when _____.

* God, thank you that you give me the security of explaining what's right and wrong. Remind me of any ways that I need to stay within the boundaries you have set. I sense that you want these changes in my life: _____.

LIVE: DO THE BIBLE

Direct your children onto the right path, and when they are older, they will not leave it.

—PROVERBS 22:6

* God, I want to be a source of your emotional security for my children. In what ways can I give them reassurance and stability? What promises need to be kept? In what ways can I be more dependable? Speak, Lord. I want to hear from you.

* Lord, I pray that I would know how to set appropriate boundaries with my child and discipline with wisdom. Give me guidance about how to discipline my child in the area of _____.

TAKE ACTION

- Make a plan to increase the closeness between you and your child. Lay the foundation for discipline and security by building a loving connection.

- Assess your plans for discipline. How can you improve instructions and increase clarity of expectations? What training or modeling is needed?

- Assess your plans for discipline. Are you clear about consequences? Do you follow through? Make any adjustments that are needed.

CLAIM HIS PROMISES

By your power I will be safe and secure; peace will be my portion.

—Psalm 55:18 TPT

Love People P-3:
A Spirit-empowered disciple loves people by discerning the relational needs of others and sharing God's love in meaningful ways.

A Spirit-Empowered Disciple

LIVES HIS MISSION

Day 25

Receive It,
Then Share It

May we tell people about the Jesus who lives in us as we live a grace-filled life in front of others.

STORIES FROM A PARENT'S HEART

No doubt you know the parable of the prodigal son. It goes something like this: The kid takes his trust fund and blows it on wine, women, and song, and winds up in a pigsty, then returns home to beg for food and employment. The most gripping scene in this biblical account is the one in which the father waits for his wayward son to return. We see the yearning on the father's face, the anxiety mixed with anticipation. Then one day, the father glances toward the road and sees his son coming home.

Reflect for a moment on your life. Have you had any "pigsty" moments? Have there been times when you were sure the Lord has had it with you, when you were scared that even begging His forgiveness wouldn't help? I certainly have. There have been plenty of times when I've just flat-out blown it—badly.

Reconnect with your feelings during your "prodigal" moments: ashamed, sad, guilty, insecure, lost, anxious, and disconnected. Now picture the scene of the prodigal—you—coming home. You're coming down the road toward home. What do you see? It's your Father, and He's running toward you with outstretched arms. His face is relieved rather than strained or angry. He reaches you, embraces you, and holds you close to tell you how much He loves you. He's proud to call you His child. He's excited to see you. His love is unending and unwavering.

What feelings would that prompt in you? Gratefulness? Amazement? Humility? That is grace—a loving Father affirming the importance of a relationship with us in spite of our behavior.

PRAY: LISTEN TO JESUS

I couldn't bear the thought of heaven without you, so I gave you the ultimate gift. Remember, my gift of grace is new every morning; it never runs out. My grace is not something in the past. I'm available every moment to help you carry life's burdens and meet its challenges. Experience and receive my grace, honor me with your thanks, and then share my grace with others (see Lamentations 3:23; Psalms 50:23; 68:19; 1 Peter 4:10).

* Jesus, I am grateful your grace is new every morning because I need more of your _____ today. I need more of your unconditional love so that _____.

* Lord, infuse me with a fresh dose of your grace for _____ (name another adult who could benefit from more of God's grace demonstrated through you). Who

needs to hear about God's grace and how it has empowered me to give?

* I especially need more of your _____ as I _____. I want to share the hope that is in me.

LIVE: DO THE BIBLE

As each one has received a special gift, employ it in serving one another as good stewards of the manifold grace of God.

—1 Peter 4:10 NASB

* God, I have received your gift of _____ (name an aspect of God's grace—forgiveness, acceptance, patience, approval, kindness, or self-control), and now I want to give it to my children. Help me demonstrate more of your grace as I _____.

* Lord, I pray that you would show our family who might need to hear the story of God's grace and how it has empowered us to give grace to one another.

TAKE ACTION

* Discuss with your children the people you know who might be experiencing some kind of life challenge or struggle. Together as a family, call or deliver a gift to this person. Surprise this person with startling love—just like the father did with the prodigal son.

- Have this conversation with your children: "I've seen Jesus make a difference in my life by _____" or, "Here's how I saw God's grace change people: _____."

CLAIM HIS PROMISES

I can do all things through him who strengthens me.

—PHILIPPIANS 4:13 ESV

Live His Mission M-1:
A Spirit-empowered disciple lives His mission by actively sharing their life with others and telling them about the Jesus who lives inside of us.

Day 26

The Zaccheus Principle

> May we tell people about the Jesus who lives in us, specifically how He empowers us to look beyond faults and see needs.

STORIES FROM A PARENT'S HEART

Zaccheus—a hated tax collector, a traitor to his own people, and a thief—was no doubt often ridiculed and attacked for his sins. Lonely and curious, he climbed a tree to get a good look at the Messiah as He passed by (see Luke 19:1–27). Zaccheus had to wonder if Jesus would notice him. And if Jesus did, would He also reject him?

What a miracle Christ's call must have been to this outcast! Our Savior asked Zaccheus to share a meal, inviting him into one of the most intimate social settings of the day. This simple invitation from Jesus was a deliberate offer of welcome, reception, and loving relationship. Jesus looked beyond the faults of Zaccheus and saw his need.

In the midst of Zaccheus' failures, Jesus offered compassion, companionship, and acceptance. It's interesting to note what Jesus *didn't* do that day: He didn't attack the tax collector's behavior, point out things that were wrong with him, or even give helpful advice. He didn't remind Zacchaeus of what he should be doing or criticize him for not taking more responsibility. Jesus didn't quote Scripture to Zacchaeus or make comparisons with other tax collectors in town. He didn't try to manipulate change in Zacchaeus or withhold affection from him.

My children and I have experienced the blessing of the Zacchaeus principle—to look beyond someone's faults and see their needs. We frequently ask God for a fresh reminder of how He has looked beyond *our* faults, and then ask His help to do the same for others.

PRAY: LISTEN TO JESUS

I came to seek and to save you! I didn't wait until you shaped up or acted right. I looked beyond your faults and loved you while you were still a sinner. The world needs my kind of love; there's too much comparison, criticism, and selfishness. Look for opportunities to share how my love for you has changed your relationship with your children (see Luke 19:1–27; Romans 5:8).

* Jesus, when I reflect on how you have looked past my faults and met my needs, I am filled with gratitude because _____. God, remind me of the awesome deeds you have done in my life and our family, particularly in how you have allowed me to look beyond faults and see needs.

* Lord, I pray that you would give our family a fresh experience of gratitude for how you have changed our relationships. Give us more insight into how you have

empowered us to look beyond one another's faults to see and meet needs.

LIVE: DO THE BIBLE

Come and see the works of God, who is awesome in His deeds toward the sons of men.

—PSALM 66:5 NASB

* God, as I have come to have this Zacchaeus perspective with my children, you have changed me and our relationship by _____. I'm thankful because _____. Who needs to hear and see these works of yours? Give me opportunities to share your deeds.

* Lord, I pray you would help my children see people's needs as well as their behavior. Give them opportunities to tell about how you do the same for us.

TAKE ACTION

• Talk with your child about how the Zacchaeus principle has been true for you and your family.

• Look for opportunities to show kindness to neighbors or friends who might be displaying behavior that's less than perfect. Talk about how Jesus does the same for us.

• Have this conversation with your child: "I wasn't always sure that people can change, but I've seen how God changes people with His love. Here's how ..."

CLAIM HIS PROMISES

And I pray that the sharing of your faith may become effective for the full knowledge of every good thing that is in us for the sake of Christ.

—Philemon 1:6 ESV

Live His Mission M-1:
A Spirit-empowered disciple lives His mission by actively sharing their life with others and telling them about the Jesus who lives inside of us.

Day 27

In Spite
of Differences

May we tell people about the Jesus who lives in us, specifically how He empowers us to love each other in spite of differences.

STORIES FROM A PARENT'S HEART

During Jesus' earthly ministry, He accepted people regardless of their differences. He cared about people regardless of their ethnicity, gender, social standing, or moral failures. He loved them unconditionally, forgave freely, and gently restored broken people to spiritual health.

One of the most powerful testimonies of God's work in our family has come out of this same challenge. We work hard to look beyond one another's faults. The closer we get to others, the more we notice their imperfections. In our family, we try to look past the other person's flaws and love in spite of those flaws. We also make a special effort to show acceptance. When a family member fails in some way or isn't as good as another person at a certain task, we try not to tease or belittle one another. These times are our opportunity to love a person anyway.

Finally, in our family, we look for people who are new or different from the group. Our priority is to include friends who are new to the school and invite people who are alone into the group. We even look for appropriate opportunities to spend time with friends or families who believe differently than we do. We want to be a family who moves toward those who are different but know that it's only Jesus who empowers us to show this kind of loving acceptance.

PRAY: LISTEN TO JESUS

Humble yourself, and I will lift you up. I love it when you acknowledge your dependence on me. I can't wait to come to your aid. I am ready to teach you my ways and lead you in how to celebrate the differences between you, your child, and others around you. Your humility is what moves me to action. I keep my distance from the proud. So talk freely about how you need me and how you are depending on me (see James 4:10; Psalms 25:9; 69:32; 138:6; Isaiah 55:8; 1 Peter 3:7).

* Jesus, please show me your ways and your thoughts. Especially when I'm tempted to think that only my ways are best, reveal your perspective. I need to specifically hear you concerning _____.

* Lord, I pray for our family. We are depending on you to help us navigate our differences. We especially need your help concerning _____.

LIVE: DO THE BIBLE

For we are God's masterpiece. He has created us anew in Christ Jesus, so we can do the good things he planned for us long ago.

—EPHESIANS 2:10

* God, I want to see my children as your masterpiece. Show me the traits about them that make you particularly proud of your creation. Show me, Lord. I am celebrating these differences about my children: _____.

* God, help my children to see other people as God's masterpiece. Help them demonstrate more loving acceptance, particularly in _____.

* Lord, you have planned good things for each of us to do. Help us celebrate our differences and point more and more people to you by sharing how _____.

TAKE ACTION

• Pray about any improvements or changes you could make that would help the environment of your family. Are there any areas where you could look beyond someone's faults, refrain from teasing, or demonstrate a gentler response to another person's failure?

• Look for an opportunity for you and your children to accept someone who is different. Look for someone new or who is not a part of the group. Pray for that person, and then plan a way to show the acceptance of Jesus in spite of their differences.

- As a family, talk about the ways that Jesus helps you accept one another's differences. Pray for an opportunity to tell others about Jesus.

CLAIM HIS PROMISES

You faithfully answer our prayers with awesome deeds, O God our savior.

—Psalm 65:5

Live His Mission M-1:
A Spirit-empowered disciple lives His mission by actively sharing his or her life with others and telling them about the Jesus who lives inside of us.

Day 28

Sharing
Our Struggles

May we tell people about the Jesus who lives in us, as we are vulnerable with our weaknesses and struggles.

STORIES FROM A PARENT'S HEART

Blended families face unique challenges. One of the ways to navigate these challenges is to set expectations appropriately. There are also many myths about stepfamilies, and one of those myths is the expectation of instant love. Just because you love your partner does not mean you'll automatically experience love with the children. We certainly had to overcome this myth and face this challenge as a blended family. It was only God who drew our family together.

It took more than seven years, but our family now has deep connections and close relationships between parents, stepparents, children, and stepchildren. Our family was born out of loss, which made our first years together pretty rocky, but Jesus brought peace to our family, stability to our relationships, and a special love for one another.

Our family's story is one of challenge, heartache, and eventual hope. It's also a story that brings encouragement to many other families. My husband and I have discovered that as we are vulnerable about the struggles of our early years and the challenges we've endured, people want to hear more. When we tell about how we've overcome the conflict and the distance of relationships, people want to know how we did it. That's when we get to tell them about Jesus. It's only because of Him that our family loves. It's only because of Him that our family thrives.

PRAY: LISTEN TO JESUS

You can put your trust in me. I am faithful and trustworthy in all I do. I am so trustworthy that I am surrounded by faithfulness. When you don't know what to do or you don't know where to turn, come to me. Let your eyes and focus be on me. I am your source. I have enough. As we walk together through the struggles of this world, we'll show others what it looks like to be my disciple. When you love one another even when it's hard, people will become convinced that I am the source of love (see 2 Corinthians 1:18–20; Psalms 33:4; 89:8; 1 Peter 3:15).

* Jesus, I am grateful that our family can trust you to _____. We don't know what to do about _____, so our eyes are on you because _____.

* Lord, remind us that you are faithful, and we can trust you to _____. Please give us a renewed focus on you even as we may not know how to _____.

LIVE: DO THE BIBLE

And if someone asks about your hope as a believer, always be ready to explain it.

—1 Peter 3:15

* God, I want our family to be able to share about our hope and trust in you. Empower us to be vulnerable about our struggle with _____ and how we trust you to _____.

* We have hope in you because _____, so give us the right words and the opportunity to share our story of hope with those who don't yet know you.

TAKE ACTION

• Talk with your child about the struggles (with age-appropriate topics) you have had in the past and how you trust in God because He brought healing, resolution, or peace.

• Talk with your family about some of your current struggles as a family and how you are trusting God. Pray together, asking for opportunities to share your testimony of hope with others.

• Start a Blessing Book. Record the struggles you face as a family and the way God answers prayer, provides, protects, encourages, and guides you. Let this book be a tangible record of your story of hope. Invite another family to dinner and share some of the entries in your Blessing Book.

CLAIM HIS PROMISES

*Depend on GOD and keep at it because in the LORD GOD you
have a sure thing.*

—ISAIAH 26:4 MSG

Live His Mission M-1:
A Spirit-empowered disciple lives His mission by actively
sharing his or her life with others and telling them about the
Jesus who lives inside of us.

Day 29

One of a Kind

May we tell people about the Jesus who lives in us as we seize opportunities that arise in our daily lives.

STORIES FROM A PARENT'S HEART

There isn't a sport that my son doesn't like to watch or play. Any game, any time. He loves the action and the adrenaline. God has blessed him with a passion for sports and an ability to play several of them well.

Over the years, we've enjoyed the special opportunity to share Jesus with many of our friends. On long road trips with the team, we've talked with other parents about the joys and challenges of raising young men of integrity. We've laughed and cried together. We've celebrated with one another when our boys made good life choices and comforted one another when they didn't.

Long weekend tournaments gave us the chance to get to know whole families. My husband has helped repair a grandmother's roof, and I've helped care for newly adopted babies so a mom could watch the game.

It's been amazing. We've seen friends come to Christ *because* of our son's interests and passion for sports. It's these regular moments that come with baseball, football, and basketball that have provided tremendous opportunities to share the love of Jesus with others.

PRAY: LISTEN TO JESUS

I've formed you with unique talents, interests, and abilities. I created you with these gifts so you can be a one-of-a-kind expression of me. I placed all these abilities in you so you can do the great things I have planned—like introduce others to me. I love to see you live out your interests and enjoy life, and I love seeing you bring my hope to this world (see Colossians 1:27).

* Jesus, when I imagine that you created me and the rest of my family to be one-of-a-kind expressions of you and that you gave us these gifts to draw others to you, I feel _____.

* Lord, remind me often that the regular moments of our day can turn into divine appointments from you. I'm wondering if you want me to see _____ as divine appointments.

LIVE: DO THE BIBLE

Let us not love in word or talk but in deed and in truth.

—1 John 3:18 ESV

* God, show me and our family the ways you would like for us to share your love in practical ways. How can we use the opportunities, gifts, and talents you give us on a daily basis to create spiritual conversations about you? Speak to me, Lord. I am listening.

＊ God, I pray you would show my children the unique opportunities you give them every day to love others and point them to you. Give my children boldness to utilize their talent in _____ to point to Jesus.

TAKE ACTION

• Talk and pray with your family about how you might work together to combine your daily interests and passions to cultivate friends who are not yet followers of Jesus. Make plans for building these friendships and sharing the love of Jesus with them.

• Discuss and plan ways for your family to turn regular moments of the day into divine opportunities for Jesus. Who could you get to know on your sports team? Who could you invite over for dinner after the kids' events? Who needs our support, encouragement, acceptance, or care as we see them on a regular basis? How will we show them the love of Jesus?

CLAIM HIS PROMISES

For I am not ashamed of the gospel, for it is the power of God for salvation to everyone who believes.

—Romans 1:16 ESV

Live His Mission M-1:
A Spirit-empowered disciple lives His mission by actively sharing his or her life with others and telling them about the Jesus who lives inside of us.

Day 30

The Art
of the Question

May we tell people about the Jesus who lives in us, specifically as we share our lives and the gospel.

STORIES FROM A PARENT'S HEART

I've discovered that I'm not very good at asking questions. I also discovered that my kids weren't great at it either. This became a problem when our family took seriously the command to share our faith. I had the motivation and sensed God's calling, and yet when it came to the practical step of starting and deepening conversations with people, I came up short.

In order to start a relationship where I had the freedom to share the gospel, I needed to know how to deepen relationships. I had to learn how to ask questions that moved our relationship from the surface to a deeper knowing of one another. Here's what I learned:

- **Slow down.** We all tend to rush past opportunities to make relational connections. So I had to slow down and take the time to *make* conversation.

- **Ask more relational questions.** We all tend to ask about facts, opinions, and information. I had to be intentional about asking about people's lives, their families, their feelings, and their needs.
- **Listen.** We all have a tendency to talk more than we listen. I had to change to learn to give my undivided attention to the people God places in my path.

These tips have helped me deepen my relationships with people. I've learned to connect with others in more meaningful ways, and God has provided incredible opportunities for me to share my life and the gospel.

PRAY: LISTEN TO JESUS

Look for people who might need you to share your life and the gospel. Begin by taking time to be with me. Next, be sure to share your life and the gospel with your spouse, children, and family. Then you'll want to share the good news with neighbors, coworkers, and people of your community. Share not only the salvation story but also the everyday blessings I bring to your life (see Matthew 28:19–20).

＊ Jesus, make me more aware of the everyday blessings you bring to my life and then give me opportunities to tell about those blessings. I want to brag on my God about _____.

＊ Lord, please make my family more aware of the every-day blessings you bring to our lives. Give my children opportunities to tell others about those blessings. Empower them to _____.

LIVE: DO THE BIBLE

We loved you so much that we shared with you not only God's Good News but our own lives, too.

—1 Thessalonians 2:8

* God, show our family the person who needs to hear your Good News and the ways you have blessed our life. Speak to me, Lord. I am listening. Give me opportunities to share the Good News and the power to proclaim it.

* Lord, please show my children the friends who need to hear about your Good News and the ways you have blessed their lives. Give my children opportunities and empowerment.

TAKE ACTION

• First, talk with your child about the ways God has made a difference in your family, then look for opportunities to tell your Jesus story to another person or family. Share how Jesus is changing you, your life, and your family as a whole.

• As needed, look for ways to connect with unchurched families. Invite them to your home, do life together, and share the hope that is within you.

CLAIM HIS PROMISES

> *Everything is from God, who reconciled us to Himself through*
> *Christ and gave us the ministry of reconciliation.*
>
> —2 Corinthians 5:18 HCSB

Live His Mission M-1:

A Spirit-empowered disciple lives His mission by actively sharing his or her life with others and telling them about the Jesus who lives inside of us.

Day 31

Kindness
Is Powerful

May we tell people about the Jesus who lives in us, especially the gospel's power of kindness.

STORIES FROM A PARENT'S HEART

Jesus tells the story of a man who is robbed and left for dead on the side of the road. Two religious men walk past the injured man without offering help, but a man from Samaria shows kindness and offers aid. The Samaritan bandages his wounds, takes him to an inn, and provides for his continued care.

What did the Samaritan man have that the religious leaders lacked? What motivated him? I think it was that the Samaritan had encountered the miraculous love of God and that he had never gotten over the wonder of God's abundant care for him. He was grateful for what God had done for him, which motivated him to care for others.

Are we still grateful for what God has done for us? Though we were still in sin, God selflessly gave His Son. Christ humbled

Himself and left heaven to become a servant on our behalf, because His provision and care were exactly what we needed. He gave forgiveness, acceptance, love, and purpose in life.

Like the Samaritan, I can become genuinely sensitive to the needs of others—particularly my children—by being mindful that I am a blessed recipient of God's abundant kindness. It's sobering to think that because of Jesus, I hold within me the kindness others need: acceptance, security, comfort, encouragement, care, and love. On the other hand, to withhold these blessings or to be insensitive to others' needs is to behave just like the religious men of the Samaritan story, who ignored the needs of the injured man and thought only of themselves.

PRAY: LISTEN TO JESUS

It will be my heart of love, expressed through my people, that will draw a searching world to ask about me. So first, remember my kindness. I have provided all the acceptance, support, and comfort you need. Spend time meditating on my kindness toward you, and then demonstrate that kindness with your family. It's great practice for sharing my kindness with others!

When people who don't know me receive some of my acceptance, encouragement, comfort, and support delivered through you, they will begin to wonder, "Where did you get all that kindness?" At that point, you'll be ready to talk about the hope that is inside you. It's their experience of kindness that opens the door for the gospel (see 1 Peter 3:15; Romans 15:7; 2:4; Galatians 6:2; 2 Corinthians 1:3–4).

* Jesus, I'm overwhelmed by your kindness toward me, specifically how you _____.

* Lord, reveal more and more ways that I have been the beneficiary of your kindness. What reminders of your kindness do you have for me?

LIVE: DO THE BIBLE

Or do you think lightly of the riches of His kindness and tolerance and patience, not knowing that the kindness of God leads you to repentance?

—ROMANS 2:4 NASB

* God, because of your kindness toward me, I want to give more of your _____ to my family. I also want to give more of your _____ to others, such as _____.

* Lord, overwhelm our family with stories of how you have enabled us to demonstrate kindness so we will have the opportunity to tell them about you.

TAKE ACTION

• Celebrate the powerful impact of kindness in your family. Talk and pray together about sharing your story with others, giving testimony of the one who is the source of your kindheartedness.

• Discuss ways to show kindness to neighbors, friends, or members of the community. Rake leaves for a neighbor. Prepare gifts for the homeless. Bring a meal to a friend

who is ill. Demonstrate kindness and then celebrate how
the Lord loved others through you.

CLAIM HIS PROMISES

*"For you will be a witness for him to everyone of what you
have seen and heard."*

—Acts 22:15 ESV

Live His Mission M-1:
A Spirit-empowered disciple lives His mission by actively
sharing his or her life with others and telling them about the
Jesus who lives inside of us.

APPENDIX 1

ABOUT THE
GREAT COMMANDMENT NETWORK

The Great Commandment Network is an international collaborative network of strategic kingdom leaders from the faith community, marketplace, education, and caregiving fields who prioritize the powerful simplicity of the words of Jesus to love God, love others, and see others become His followers (Matthew 22:37–40, Matthew 28:19–20).

THE GREAT COMMANDMENT NETWORK IS SERVED THROUGH THE FOLLOWING:

Relationship Press – This team collaborates, supports, and joins together with churches, denominational partners, and professional associates to develop, print, and produce resources that facilitate ongoing Great Commandment ministry.

The Center for Relational Leadership – Their mission is to teach, train, and mentor both ministry and corporate leaders in Great Commandment principles, seeking to equip leaders with relational skills so they might lead as Jesus led.

The Galatians 6:6 Retreat Ministry – This ministry offers a unique two-day retreat for ministers and their spouses for personal renewal and for reestablishing and affirming ministry and family priorities.

The Center for Relational Care (CRC) – The CRC provides therapy and support to relationships in crisis through an accelerated process of growth and healing, including Relational Care Intensives for couples, families, and singles.

For more information on how you, your church, ministry, denomination, or movement can be served by the Great Commandment Network write or call:

Great Commandment Network
2511 South Lakeline Blvd.
Cedar Park, Texas 78613
#800-881-8008
Or visit our website: www.GreatCommandment.net

APPENDIX 2

A SPIRIT-EMPOWERED FAITH

Expresses Itself in Great Commission Living Empowered by Great Commandment Love

**begins with the end in mind:
The Great Commission calls us
to make disciples.**

"Go therefore and make disciples of all the nations, baptizing them in the name of the Father and the Son and the Holy Spirit teaching them to observe all things that I have commanded you; and lo, I am with you always, even to the end of the age." (Matthew 28:19–20)

The ultimate goal of our faith journey is to relate to the person of Jesus, because it is our relational connection to Jesus that will produce Christ-likeness and spiritual growth. This relational perspective of discipleship is required if we hope to have a faith that is marked by the Spirit's power.

Models of discipleship that are based solely upon what we *know* and what we *do* are incomplete, lacking the empowerment of a life of loving and living intimately with Jesus. **A Spirit-empowered faith is relational and impossible to realize apart from a special work of the Spirit.** For example, the Spirit-empowered outcome of "listening to and hearing God" implies relationship—it is both relational in focus and requires the Holy Spirit's power to live.

**begins at the right place:
The Great Commandment calls us to
start with loving God and loving others.**

"'You shall love the LORD your God with all your heart, with all your soul, and with all your mind.' This is the first and great commandment. And the second is like it: 'You shall love your neighbor as yourself.' On these two commandments hang all the Law and the Prophets."

(Matthew 22:37–40)

Relevant discipleship does not begin with doctrines or teaching, parables or stewardship—but with loving the Lord with all your heart, mind, soul, and strength and then loving the people closest to you. Since Matthew 22:37–40 gives us the first and greatest commandment, *a Spirit-empowered faith starts where the Great Commandment tells us to start: A disciple must first learn to deeply love the Lord and to express His love to the "nearest ones"—his or her family, church, and community (and in that order).*

 embraces a relational process of Christlikeness.

Scripture reminds us that there are three sources of light for our journey: Jesus, His Word, and His people. The process of discipleship (or becoming more like Jesus) occurs as we relate intimately with each source of light.

"Walk while you have the light, lest darkness overtake you." (John 12:35)

Spirit-empowered discipleship will require a lifestyle of:
- Fresh encounters with Jesus (John 8:12)
- Frequent experiences of Scripture (Psalm 119:105)
- Faithful engagement with God's people (Matthew 5:14)

 can be defined with observable outcomes using a biblical framework.

The metrics for measuring Spirit-empowered faith or the growth of a disciple come from Scripture and are organized/framed around four distinct dimensions of a disciple who serves.

And He Himself gave some to be apostles, some prophets,
some evangelists, and some pastors and teachers,
for the equipping of the saints for the work of ministry,
for the edifying of the body of Christ.
(Ephesians 4:11–12)

A relational framework for organizing Spirit-Empowered Discipleship Outcomes draws from a cluster analysis of several Greek (*diakoneo, leitourgeo, douleuo*) and Hebrew words (*'abad, Sharat*), which elaborate on the Ephesians 4:12 declaration that Christ's followers are to be equipped for works of ministry or service. Therefore, the 40 Spirit-Empowered Faith Outcomes have been identified and organized around:

* Serving/loving the Lord – *While they were* **ministering** *to the Lord and fasting* (Acts 13:2 NASB).[1]
* Serving/loving the Word – *But we will devote ourselves to prayer and to the* **ministry** *of the word* (Acts 6:4 NASB).[2]
* Serving/loving people – *Through love* **serve** *one another* (Galatians 5:13 NASB).[3]
* Serving/loving His mission – *Now all these things are from God, who reconciled us to Himself through Christ and gave us the* **ministry** *of reconciliation* (2 Corinthians 5:18 NASB).[4]

---

1 Ferguson, David L. *Great Commandment Principle*. Cedar Park, Texas: Relationship Press, 2013.

2 Ferguson, David L. *Relational Foundations*. Cedar Park, Texas: Relationship Press, 2004.

3 Ferguson, David L. *Relational Discipleship*. Cedar Park, Texas: Relationship Press, 2005.

4 "Spirit Empowered Outcomes," www.empowered21.com, Empowered 21 Global Council, http://empowered21.com/discipleship-materials/.

A SPIRIT-EMPOWERED DISCIPLE LOVES THE LORD THROUGH

L1. Practicing thanksgiving in all things
Enter into His gates with thanksgiving (Ps. 100:4). *In everything give thanks* (1 Th. 5:18). *As sorrowful, yet always rejoicing* (2 Cor. 6:10).

L2. Listening to and hearing God for direction and discernment
"Speak, Lord, for Your servant hears" (1 Sam. 3:8–9). *Mary, who also sat at Jesus' feet and heard His word* (Lk. 10:38–42). *And the Lord said, "Shall I hide from Abraham what I am doing … ?"* (Gen. 18:17). *But as the same anointing teaches you concerning all things …* (1 Jn. 2:27).

L3. Experiencing God as He really is through deepened intimacy with Him
"Hear, O Israel: The Lord our God, the Lord is one! You shall love the Lord your God with all your heart, with all your soul, and with all your strength" (Deut. 6:4–5). *Therefore the Lord will wait, that He may be gracious to you; and therefore He will be exalted, that He may have mercy on you. For the Lord is a God of justice …* (Is. 30:18). See also John 14:9.

L4. Rejoicing regularly in my identity as "His Beloved"
And his banner over me was love (Song of Sol. 2:4). *To the praise of the glory of His grace, by which He made us accepted in the Beloved* (Eph. 1:6). *For so He gives His beloved sleep* (Ps. 127:2).

L5. Living with a passionate longing for purity and to please Him in all things
Who may ascend into the hill of the Lord? … He who has clean hands and a pure heart (Ps. 24:3–4). *Beloved, let us cleanse ourselves from all filthiness of flesh and spirit, perfecting holiness in the fear of God* (2 Cor. 7:1). *"I always do those things that please Him"* (Jn. 8:29). *"Though He slay me, yet will I trust Him"* (Job 13:15).

L6.   Consistent practice of self-denial, fasting, and solitude rest
He turned and said to Peter, "Get behind me, Satan! You are offense to Me, for you are not mindful of the things of God, but the things of men" (Mt. 16:23). "But you, when you fast …" (Mt. 6:17). "Be still, and know that I am God" (Ps. 46:10).

L7.   Entering often into Spirit-led praise and worship
Bless the LORD, O my soul, and all that is within me (Ps. 103:1). Serve the LORD with fear (Ps. 2:11). I thank You, Father, Lord of heaven and earth (Mt. 11:25).

L8.   Disciplined, bold, and believing prayer
Praying always with all prayer and supplication in the Spirit (Eph. 6:18). "Call to Me, and I will answer you" (Jer. 33:3). If we ask anything according to His will, He hears us. And if we know that He hears us, whatever we ask, we know that we have the petitions that we have asked of Him (1 Jn. 5:14–15).

L9.   Faithful stewardship and exercise of the gifts of the Spirit for empowered living and sacrifice
By one Spirit we were all baptized into one body—whether Jews or Greeks, whether slaves or free—and have all been made to drink into one Spirit (1 Cor. 12:13). "But you shall receive power when the Holy Spirit has come upon you" (Acts 1:8). But the manifestation of the Spirit is given to each one for the profit of all (1 Cor. 12:7). See also 1 Pet. 4:10 and Rom. 12:6.

L10.   Practicing the presence of the Lord, yielding to the Spirit's work of Christlikeness
But we all, with unveiled face, … are being transformed into the same from glory to glory, just as by the Spirit of the Lord (2 Cor. 3:18). As the deer pants for the water brooks, so pants my soul after You, O God (Ps. 42:1).

A SPIRIT-EMPOWERED DISCIPLE LIVES THE WORD THROUGH

W1. Frequently being led by the Spirit into deeper love for the One who wrote the Word

" 'You shall love the Lord your God … .' 'You shall love neighbor as yourself.' On these two commandments hang all the Law and the Prophets" (Mt. 22:37–40). *And I will delight myself in Your commandments, which I love.* (Ps. 119:47). *"The fear of the* Lord *is clean … . More to be desired are they than gold … sweeter also than honey"* (Ps. 19:9–10).

W2. Being a "living epistle" in reverence and awe as His Word becomes real in my life, vocation, and calling

You are our epistle written in our hearts, known and read by all men (2 Cor. 3:2). *And the Word became flesh and dwelt among us* (Jn. 1:14). *Husbands, love your wives … cleanse her with the washing of water by the word* (Eph. 5:25–26). *See also Tit. 2:5. And whatever you do, do it heartily, as to the Lord and not to men* (Col. 3:23).

W3. Yielding to the Scripture's protective cautions and transforming power to bring life change in me

Through Your precepts I get understanding; therefore I hate every false way (Ps. 119:104). *"Let it be to me according to your word"* (Lk. 1:38). *How can a young man cleanse his way? By taking heed according to Your word* (Ps. 119:9). See also Col. 3:16–17.

W4. Humbly and vulnerably sharing of the Spirit's transforming work through the Word

I will speak of your testimonies also before kings, and will not be ashamed (Ps. 119:46). *Preach the word! Be ready in season and out of season* (2 Tim. 4:2).

W5. Meditating consistently on more and more of the Word hidden in the heart

Your word I have hidden in my heart, that I might not sin against You (Ps. 119:11). *Let the words of my mouth and the meditation of my heart be acceptable in Your sight, O LORD, my strength and my Redeemer* (Ps. 19:14).

W6. Encountering Jesus in the Word for deepened transformation in Christlikeness

But we all, with unveiled face, … are being transformed into the same image from glory to glory, just as by the Spirit of the Lord (2 Cor. 3:18). *If you abide in Me, and My words abide in you, you will ask what you desire, and it shall be done for you* (Jn. 15:7). See also Lk. 24:32, Ps. 119:136, and 2 Cor. 1:20.

W7. A life explained as one of "experiencing Scripture"

But this is what was spoken by the prophet Joel (Acts 2:16). *This is my comfort in my affliction, for Your word has given me life* (Ps. 119:50). *My soul breaks with longing for Your judgements at all times* (Ps. 119:20).

W8. Living "naturally supernatural" in all of life as His Spirit makes the written Word (*logos*) the living Word (*rhema*)

*So then aith comes by hearing, and hearing by the word (*rhema*) of God* (Rom. 10:17). *Your word is a lamp to my feet and a light to my path* (Ps. 119:105).

W9. Living abundantly "in the present" as His Word brings healing to hurt and anger, guilt, fear, and condemnation—which are heart hindrances to life abundant

"The thief does not come except to steal, and to kill, and to destroy" (Jn. 10:10). *I will run the course of Your commandments, for You shall enlarge my heart* (Ps. 119:32). *"And you shall know the truth, and the truth shall make you free"* (Jn. 8:32). *Stand fast therefore in the liberty by which Christ has made us free, and do not be entangled again with a yoke of bondage* (Gal. 5:1).

W10. Implicit, unwavering trust that His Word will never fail
"The grass withers, the flower fades, but the word of our God stands forever" (Is. 40:8). *"So shall My word be that goes forth from My mouth; it shall not return to Me void"* (Is. 55:11).

A SPIRIT-EMPOWERED DISCIPLE LOVES PEOPLE THROUGH

P1. Living a Spirit-led life of doing good in all of life: relationships and vocation, community and calling
Who went about doing good ... (Acts 10:38). *"Let your light so shine before men, that they may see your good works and glorify your Father in heaven"* (Mt. 5:16). *"But love your enemies, do good, and lend, hoping for nothing in return; and your reward will be great, and you will be sons of the Most High. For He is kind to the unthankful and evil"* (Lk. 6:35). See also Rom. 15:2.

P2. "Startling people" with loving initiatives to "give first"
"Give, and it will be given to you: good measure, pressed down, shaken together, and running over will be put into your bosom" (Lk. 6:38). *Then Jesus said, "Father, forgive them, for they do not know what they do"* (Lk. 23:34). See also Lk. 23:43 and Jn. 19:27.

P3. Discerning the relational needs of others with a heart to give of His love
Let no corrupt word proceed out of your mouth, but what is good for necessary edification, that it might impart grace to the hearers (Eph. 4:29). *And my God shall supply all your need according to His riches in glory by Christ Jesus* (Phil. 4:19). See also Lk. 6:30.

P4. Seeing people as needing BOTH redemption from sin AND intimacy in relationships, addressing both human fallen-ness and aloneness
But God demonstrates His own love toward us, in that while we were still sinners, Christ died for us (Rom. 5:8). *And when Jesus came to the place, He looked up and saw him, and said to him, "Zacchaeus, make haste and come down, for today I must stay at your house"* (Lk. 19:5). See also Mk. 8:24 and Gen. 2:18.

P5. Ministering His life and love to our nearest ones at home and with family as well as faithful engagement in His body, the church
Husbands, likewise, dwell with them with understanding, giving honor to the wife, as to the weaker vessel, and as being heirs together of the grace of life, that your prayers may not be hindered (1 Pet. 3:7). See also 1 Pet. 3:1 and Ps. 127:3.

P6. Expressing the fruit of the Spirit as a lifestyle and identity
But the fruit of the Spirit is love, joy, peace, longsuffering, kindness, goodness, faithfulness, gentleness, self-control (Gal. 5:22–23). *A man's stomach shall be satisfied from the fruit of his mouth; From the produce of his lips he shall be filled* (Prov. 18:20).

P7. Expecting and demonstrating the supernatural as His spiritual gifts are made manifest and His grace is at work by His Spirit
In mighty signs and wonders, by the power of the Spirit of God, so that from Jerusalem and round about to Illyricum I have fully preached the gospel of Christ (Rom. 15:19). *"Most assuredly, I say to you, he who believes in Me, the works that I do he will do also"* (Jn. 14:12). See also 1 Cor. 14:1.

P8. Taking courageous initiative as a peacemaker, reconciling relationships along life's journey
Be at peace among yourselves (1 Th. 5:13). *For He Himself is our peace, who has made both one, and has broken down the middle wall of separation* (Eph. 2:14). *Confess your trespasses to one another, and pray for one another, that you may be healed* (Jas. 5:16).

P9. Demonstrating His love to an ever growing network of "others" as He continues to challenge us to love "beyond our comfort"

He who says, "I know Him," and does not keep His commandments, is a liar, and the truth is not in him (1 Jn. 2:4). *If someone says, "I love God," and hates his brother, he is a liar; for he who does not love his brother whom he has seen, how can he love God whom he has not seen?* (1 Jn. 4:20).

P10. Humbly acknowledging to the Lord, ourselves, and others that it is Jesus in and through us who is loving others at their point of need

"Take My yoke upon you and learn from Me, for I am gentle and lowly in heart, and you will find rest for your souls" (Mt. 11:29). *"If I then, your Lord and Teacher, have washed your feet, you also ought to wash one another's feet"* (Jn. 13:14).

A SPIRIT-EMPOWERED DISCIPLE LIVES HIS MISSION THROUGH

M1. Imparting the gospel and one's very life in daily activities and relationships, vocation and community

So, affectionately longing for you, we were well pleased to impart to you not only the gospel of God, but also our own lives, because you had become dear to us (1 Th. 2:8–9). See also Eph. 6:19.

M2. Expressing and extending the kingdom of God as compassion, justice, love, and forgiveness are shared

"I must preach the kingdom of God to the other cities also, because for this purpose I have been sent" (Lk. 4:43). *"As You sent Me into the world, I also have sent them into the world"* (Jn. 17:18). *Restore to me the joy of Your salvation, and uphold me by Your generous Spirit. Then I will teach transgressors Your ways, and sinners shall be converted to You* (Ps. 51:12–13). See also Mic. 6:8.

M3. Championing Jesus as the only hope of eternal life and abundant living

"Nor is there salvation in any other, for there is no other name under heaven given among men by which we must be saved" (Acts 4:12). *"The thief does not come except to steal, and to kill, and to destroy. I have come so that they may have life, and that they have it more abundantly"* (Jn. 10:10). See also Acts 4:12 and Jn. 14:6.

M4. Yielding to the Spirit's role to convict others as He chooses, resisting expressions of condemnation

"And when He has come, He will convict the world of sin, and of righteousness, and of judgment" (Jn. 16:8). *Who is he who condemns? It is Christ who died, and furthermore is also risen, who is even at the right hand of God, who also makes intercession for us* (Rom. 8:34). See also Rom. 8:1.

M5. Ministering His life and love to the "least of these"

"Then He will answer them saying, 'Assuredly, I say to you inasmuch as you did not do it to one of the least of these, you did not do it to Me'" (Mt. 25:45). *Pure and undefiled religion before God and the Father is this: to visit orphans and widows in their trouble, and to keep oneself unspotted from the world* (Jas. 1:27).

M6. Bearing witness of a confident peace and expectant hope in God's lordship in all things

Now may the Lord of peace Himself give you peace always in every way. The Lord be with you all (2 Thess. 3:16). *And let the peace of God rule in your hearts, to which also you were called in one body; and be thankful* (Col. 3:15). See also Rom. 8:28 and Ps. 146:5.

M7. Faithfully sharing of time, talent, gifts, and resources in furthering His mission

Of which I became a minister according to the stewardship from God which was given to me for you, to fulfill the word of God (Col. 1:25). *"For everyone to whom much is given, from him much will be required"* (Lk. 12:48). See also 1 Cor. 4:1–2.

M8.   Attentive listening to others' story, vulnerably sharing of our story, and a sensitive witness of Jesus' story as life's ultimate hope; developing your story of prodigal, preoccupied and pain-filled living; listening for others' story and sharing Jesus' story

But sanctify the Lord God in your hearts, and always be ready to give a defense to everyone who asks you a reason for the hope that is in you, with meekness and fear (1 Pet. 3:15). *"For this my son was dead and is alive again"* (Luke 15:24). See also Mk. 5:21–42 and Jn. 9:1–35.

M9.   Pouring our life into others, making disciples who in turn make disciples of others

"Go therefore and make disciples of all the nations, baptizing them in the name of the Father and of the Son and of the Holy Spirit, teaching them to observe all things that I commanded you; and lo, I am with you always, even to the end of the age" (Mt. 28:19–20). See also 2 Tim. 2:2.

M10. Living submissively within His body, the Church, as instruction and encouragement; reproof and correction are graciously received by faithful disciples

Submitting to one another in the fear of God (Eph. 5:21). *Brethren, if a man is overtaken in any trespass, you who are spiritual restore such a one in a spirit of gentleness, considering yourself lest you also be tempted* (Gal. 6:1). See also Gal. 6:2.

More 31 Days of Prayer Resources

Jesus is praying and He invites you to join Him! Lean in to listen and experience His heart for your pastor, spouse, and nation. These resources provide:

- True stories to understand opportunities for prayer.

- A powerful, Scripture-based prayer strategy for better loving the Lord, living God's Word, loving people, and living His mission.

- Scriptures, prayers, and promises to declare over your pastor, spouse, and nation.

- A practical resource for personal devotions, small group studies, and other ministries.

Order at:
GreatCommandment.net/resource-store

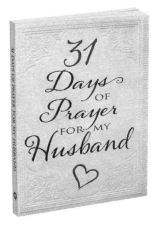

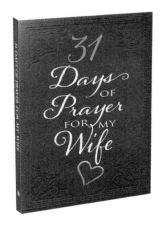

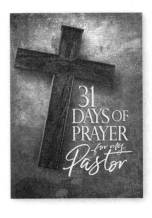

Prayer Resource Kits:

31 DAYS OF PRAYER FOR MY WIFE

This resource kit is a great tool that can be used for small group and one-on-one discipleship. Use this resource kit to make disciples who in turn make disciples.

- 8 copies of the book, *31 Days of Prayer for My Wife*
- The Spirit-Empowered Faith set:
  - A brochure explaining the Spirit-Empowered Faith content
  - 40 outcomes of a Spirit-Empowered disciple of Jesus
  - Self-Assessment tool to measure the 40 outcomes in your own life and those in your small group
  - Teaching notes on the Spirit-Empowered Faith that can be used as sermon guides or leader notes
- 2 copies of the year-long couple's devotional book, *Never Alone*.
  - One copy comes in leather and the other in paperback form
- 2 Date Night Menus – topical questions and conversations to have with your spouse on a date night around the themes of relational needs.

31 DAYS OF PRAYER FOR MY HUSBAND

This resource kit is a great tool that can be used for small group and one-on-one discipleship. Use this resource kit to make disciples who in turn make disciples.

- 8 copies of the book, *31 Days of Prayer For My Husband*
- The Spirit-Empowered Faith set:
  - A brochure explaining the Spirit-Empowered Faith content
  - 40 outcomes of a Spirit-Empowered disciple of Jesus
  - Self-Assessment tool to measure the 40 outcomes in your own life and those in your small group
  - Teaching notes on the Spirit-Empowered Faith that can be used as sermon guides or leader notes
- 2 copies of the year-long couple's devotional book, *Never Alone.*
  - One copy comes in leather and the other in paperback form
- 2 Date Night Menus – topical questions and conversations to have with your spouse on a date night around the themes of relational needs.

31 DAYS OF PRAYER FOR MY PASTOR

This resource kit is a great tool that can be used for small group and one-on-one discipleship. It's also perfect for pastor prayer teams. Use this resource kit to make disciples who in turn make disciples.

- 8 copies of the book, *31 Days of Prayer for My Pastor*
- The Spirit-Empowered Faith set:
  - A brochure explaining the Spirit-Empowered Faith content
  - 40 outcomes of a Spirit-Empowered disciple of Jesus
  - Self-Assessment tool to measure the 40 outcomes in your own life and those in your small group
  - Teaching notes on the Spirit-Empowered Faith that can be used as sermon guides or leader notes
- 2 copies of the book, *Lift Your Pastor*
- *50 Ways to Bless Your Pastor* flyer

31 DAYS OF PRAYER FOR MY NATION

This resource kit is a great tool that can be used for small group and one-on-one discipleship. Use this resource kit to make disciples who in turn make disciples.

- 8 copies of the book, *31 Days of Prayer for My Nation*
- 4 sermons built on the book's content and theme
- The Spirit-Empowered Faith set:
    - A brochure explaining the Spirit-Empowered Faith content
    - 40 outcomes of a Spirit-Empowered disciple of Jesus
    - Self-Assessment tool to measure the 40 outcomes in your own life and those in your small group
    - Teaching notes on the Spirit-Empowered Faith that can be used as sermon guides or leader notes
- 8 copies of the book, *Praying for a Christ Awakening*

31 DAYS OF PRAYER FOR MY CHILDREN

This resource kit is a great tool that can be used for small group and one-on-one discipleship. Use this resource kit to make disciples who in turn make disciples.

- 8 copies of the book, *31 Days of Prayer for My Children*
- The Spirit-Empowered Faith set:
  - A brochure explaining the Spirit-Empowered Faith content
  - 40 outcomes of a Spirit-Empowered disciple of Jesus
  - Self-Assessment tool to measure the 40 outcomes in your own life and those in your small group
  - Teaching notes on the Spirit-Empowered Faith that can be used as sermon guides or leader notes
- 1 copy of the book, *Parenting with Intimacy*
- 1 copy of the book, *Intimate Family Moments*
- A set of "Table Talk" conversations to have with your kids around the dinner table